Barton Fink

Miller's Crossing

Barton Fink
Miller's Crossing

JOEL COEN AND ETHAN COEN

Introduction
by Roderick Jaynes

ff

Faber and Faber

Boston • London

Library of Congress Cataloging-in-Publication Data

Coen, Joel.
    [Barton Fink]
    Barton Fink : Miller's Crossing / Joel Coen and Ethan Coen ;
introduction by Roderick Jaynes.
        p.   cm.
    Screenplays for the motion pictures Barton Fink and Miller's Crossing.
    ISBN 0-571-12925-0 (pbk.) : $13.95
    1. Motion picture plays. I. Coen, Ethan. II. Coen, Joel.
Miller's Crossing. 1991. III. Barton Fink (Motion picture)
IV. Miller's Crossing (Motion picture) V. Title. VI. Title: Barton
Fink. VIII. Title: Miller's Crossing.
PN1997.B217   1991
791.43'75z-dc20   91-20388
                                                                      CIP

Contents

Ethan Coen and Joel Coen on the set of MILLER'S CROSSING.
(photo by Patti Perret)

INTRODUCTION

When Joel and Ethan Coen first approached me in the autumn of 1983 to cut *Blood Simple*, it had been almost thirty years since I had last worked in film. That was on a largely forgettable entertainment called *The Mad Weekend* with Alistair Sim and Basil Radford and directed by Geoffrey Milestone. Geoff was a small man both in stature and talent and was known, rather uncharitably, both at Ealing and at Rank, as "the wee McKendrick." Still, he seemed pleased enough with my work and introduced me to a friend of his, the American director George Marshall, who was about to begin shooting *Beyond Mombassa*.

At George's suggestion I moved to New York, took an apartment, and worked for less than a week on the picture before Marshall decided that my cutting was "too damned Prussian" and replaced me with Jack Tuttle. Due to a union rule my name remained on the film while Jack went on to make a mess of things; he was a dear man but no editor, and this brings me back to the Coens. They were huge fans of *Beyond Mombassa* and wanted me to cut their first picture. I explained my involvement in the Marshall film and didn't hear from them again for several weeks, when Ethan called to inform me that Jack Tuttle had passed away in 1962 whilst cutting another Coen favorite, *Operation Fort Petticoat*. The boys glumly reiterated their offer.

I decided to accept, with mixed feelings due to the circumstances, and under two conditions: that I be left alone in the cutting room, and that I not be asked to read the script before starting in cutting. Since, throughout my career, this second condition has been the subject of some contention, I shall try to explain it here.

I've never thought much of the motion picture scenario. It has its uses, I suppose, as a rough sort of guide to the actual shooting of a movie – and of course the thesps need a *vade mecum* from which to memorize their lines. But beyond this, the utility or interest of a motion picture script seems nil. It is not a literary artifact, not having been written for publication and therefore never attracting the grade of author who would merit it. Scenarists are inevitably amateurs, boobies, and hacks. Their scripts are invariably shoddily bound and shot right through with errors of spelling and punctuation—not to speak of the lapses of taste. At best the scriptwriter is a student of writing rather than a writer *per se;* he is like a child scraping away at his scales on the violin. No sensible person would listen to this grating chatter by election, and I am far too old to feign enthusiam for such recitals. As for whatever information is required for film editing, the script contains no more than the footage itself—less, in fact. The footage will sort itself out for the discerning editor, and those of us who understand the art of the image juxtaposed need not concern ourselves with the original intent of the chap—frequently a nephew of the producer—whose scribblings give us, at many times remove, our raw material. No, it is the organization of moving images that is the very art of cinema, and true authorship resides in the hand that wields not the pen, but the razor.

Given a free hand on *Blood Simple*, I was rather proud of my first cut, but when I screened it for the lads they responded to the action scenes with silence and to the dramatic scenes with their alarming asthmatic laughter. They took the picture away and, along with a friend of theirs named Don Wiegmann, made rather a mess of things I'm afraid, but due to union rules my name remains on the picture.

I didn't hear from them after the screening and had to see the finished film two years later at the local cine in Hove, so I was surprised to get the call to cut their second effort, *Raising Arizona*. It was from Joel this time, who went to great—one might say sickening—lengths to assure me that they had got on with me personally and respected me professionally, but this time their offer was conditional on my reading their script before commencing work. The script might give me, Joel said, a fix on which characters were central and which peripheral,

x

and a firmer grasp of the order of the individual scenes. Michael Balcon had given me much the same speech before booting me off *The Bells of Rhymney's* and it had sounded no more persuasive then. So once again an opportunity foundered upon this point which I still considered a matter of principle; I turned down the lads' offer and also their next, for *Miller's Crossing*, which bore the same condition. No regrets.

I must say, however, that in watching that picture I was struck that the lads had matured somewhat. There was less of the bellowing and rum carryings-on that had so branded *Raising Arizona* the work of amateurs; the actors had been issued proper suits, the settings had been designed with a measure of restraint, and the characters spoke in a normal tone of voice and were sensibly covered in medium shots instead of the leering close-ups I had been given on *Blood Simple*. There were even frequent over-the-shoulder shots. I like an over-the-shoulder; it lets you know that the other fellow is still in the room and hasn't wandered off to do God knows what. Yes, all told the lads' third picture seemed a step up, if from an abysm.

I'm not sure why the Coens called me on their fourth picture, *Barton Fink;* our last conversation had ended with sharp words on both sides. At any rate, they were still asking me to work on condition of reading the script, which was still an impossibility; at this juncture, however, I made the concession of allowing them to tell me the story of the picture before I started work. This left them satisfied if not pleased, and they proceeded to narrate a tale which, to my mind, seemed crushingly tedious. I kept my impressions to myself though, as I attach little importance to scenario, and agreed to do the job, the more since I learned that their cinematographer would be Roger Deakins. Deakins I knew to be an able chap of good family in Chiswick (I had the good fortune to be acquainted with his gran) and I assumed that under his steadying hand the Coens would carry on with restraint.

T'would not be so. The footage I was given marked a return to the Borstal sensibility of the boys' earlier efforts — entire scenes covered without a proper camera angle, tattiness of setting and wardrobe, and actors once again encouraged to bellow and banshee. I made what sense I could of the footage, of which more later, but the strange sequel to my relationship with the Coens was that they asked me to write this introduction to the published scripts of *Miller's Crossing* and *Barton Fink*. I accepted only when they agreed not to review my remarks prior to their publication here. This I demanded on suspicion that they were soliciting my thoughts merely because they found it amusing to have their scenarios introduced by someone who had never read them, and if such were the case, I intended to disappoint them. For I then judged it a matter of principle to read the scripts, it being absurd to comment upon them otherwise, however banal I might precognosce them to be. Upon dancing through the two scenarios, though, I was surprised to discover something of interest.

Certainly neither manuscript caused me to revise my low opinion of the scriptwriting form. However, what is odd and even unique in the case of the Coens' scripts is that, inept though they may be, in my judgment they prove superior to the films based upon them. The malformed thoughts contained in the scripts that follow are at least here intercepted prior to their being mucked about by the silliness of the Coens' camera work. The *Miller's Crossing* scenario, whilst unable to propose concrete solutions to the problems of mobsterism and the bootlegging of alcohol in the 1920s, at least raises those challenging issues. And *Barton Fink* contains clever insights on certain artistical and Semitic themes. Pity that these somewhat promising beginnings should be so brutally strangled by their own parents. And by, I might add, the palsied hand of the film editor.

But I did not complete my account of my work on *Barton Fink*. At the outset the Coens were once again as good as their word, leaving me alone to impose what order I could on their unruly footage. But when I showed them my first cut, the screening ended in silence, and finally all they could find to say was that they'd been hoping for an editing style more along the lines of *Beyond Mombassa*. I gritted my teeth and explained to them – again – the nature of my involvement in that film. Perhaps my irritation showed; I am a film editor, after all, and not a diplomat or nuncio. At any rate, after the picture was taken away the Coens fiddled it with a friend of theirs, Michael Berenbaum. Perhaps the lads just wanted a bit more of the Hebrew point of view. I myself don't care for what they've done, and don't recognize much of my own in the picture now, save for my name in the credits – the good old rules and regs.

Roderick Jaynes
Hayward's Heath, Sussex
April, 1991

Barton Fink

Barton Fink was first shown at the Cannes Film Festival on May 20, 1991.

The cast included:

BARTON FINK	John Turturro
CHARLIE MEADOWS	John Goodman
AUDREY TAYLOR	Judy Davis
JACK LIPNICK	Michael Lerner
W. P. MAYHEW	John Mahoney
BEN GEISLER	Tony Shalhoub
LOU BREEZE	Jon Polito
CHET	Steve Buscemi
GARLAND STANFORD	David Warrilow
DETECTIVE MASTRIONOTTI	Richard Portnow
DETECTIVE DEUTSCH	Christopher Murney
DEREK	I. M. Hobson
POPPY CARNAHAN	Megan Faye
RICHARD ST. CLAIRE	Lance Davis
PETE	Harry Bugin
MAITRE D'	Anthony Gordon
STAGEHAND	Jack Denbo
CLAPPER BOY	Max Grodénchik
REFEREE	Robert Beecher
WRESTLER	Darwyn Swalve
GEISLER'S SECRETARY	Gayle Vance
SAILOR	Johnny Judkins
USO GIRL	Jana Marie Hupp
BEAUTY	Isabelle Townsend

And Featuring the Golden Throat of   William Preston Robertson

Directed by	Joel Coen
Produced by	Ethan Coen
Written by	Ethan Coen and Joel Coen
Co-Producer	Graham Place

2

Executive Producers	Ben Barenholtz, Ted Pedas, Jim Pedas, Bill Durkin
Director of Photography	Roger Deakins
Production Designer	Dennis Gassner
Costume Designer	Richard Hornung
Music Composed by	Carter Burwell
Edited by	Roderick Jaynes
Associate Editor	Michael Berenbaum
Supervising Sound Editor	Skip Lievsay
Dialogue Supervisor	Philip Stockton
Casting by	Donna Isaacson, C.S.A. & John Lyons, C.S.A.

3

FADE IN:

ON BARTON FINK

He is a bespectacled man in his thirties, hale but somewhat bookish. He stands, tuxedoed, in the wings of a theater, looking out at the stage, listening intently to the end of a performance.

In the shadows behind him an old stagehand leans against a flat, expressionlessly smoking a cigarette, one hand on a thick rope that hangs from the ceiling.

The voices of the performing actors echo in from the offscreen stage:

> ACTOR

I'm blowin' out of here, blowin' for good. I'm kissin' it all goodbye, these four stinkin' walls, the six flights up, the el that roars by at three A.M. like a cast-iron wind. Kiss 'em goodbye for me, Maury! I'll miss 'em—like hell I will!

> ACTRESS

Dreaming again!

> ACTOR

Not this time, Lil! I'm awake now, awake for the first time in years. Uncle Dave said it: Daylight is a dream if you've lived with your eyes closed. Well my eyes are open now! I see that choir, and I know they're dressed in rags! But we're part of that choir, both of us—yeah, and you, Maury, and Uncle Dave too!

> MAURY

The sun's coming up, kid. They'll be hawking the fish down on Fulton Street.

> ACTOR

Let 'em hawk. Let 'em sing their hearts out.

> MAURY

That's it, kid. Take that ruined choir. Make it sing!

5

ACTOR

So long, Maury.

MAURY

So long.

We hear a door open and close, then approaching footsteps. A tall, dark actor in a used tweed suit and carrying a beat-up valise passes in front of Barton.

From the offscreen stage:

MAURY

We'll hear from that kid. And I don't mean a postcard.

The actor sets the valise down and then stands waiting in the shadows behind Barton.

An older man in work clothes—not wardrobe—passes in front of Barton from the other direction, pauses at the edge of the stage and cups his hands to his mouth.

OLDER MAN

FISH! FRESH FISH!

As the man walks back off screen:

LILY

Let's spit on our hands and get to work. It's late, Maury.

MAURY

Not any more, Lil . . .

Barton mouths the last line in sync with the offscreen actor:

. . . It's early.

With this the stagehand behind Barton furiously pulls the rope hand-over-hand and we hear thunderous applause and shouts of "Bravo!"

As the stagehand finishes bringing the curtain down, somewhat muting the applause, the backstage actor trots out of frame toward the stage.

The stagehand pulls on an adjacent rope, bringing the curtain back up and unmuting the tumultuous applause.

Barton Fink seems dazed. He has been joined by two other men, both dressed in tuxedos, both beaming broadly toward the stage.

BARTON'S POV

Looking across a tenement set at the backs of the cast as the curtain rises on the enthusiastic house. The actors take their bows and the cry of "Author, Author" goes up from the crowd.

The actors turn to smile at Barton in the wings.

BARTON

He hesitates, unable to take it all in.

He is gently nudged toward the stage by the two tuxedoed gentlemen.

As he exits toward the stage the applause is deafening.

TRACKING SHOT

Pushing a maitre d' who looks back over his shoulder as he leads the way through the restaurant.

MAITRE D'
Your table is ready, Monsieur Fink . . . several members of your party have already arrived . . .

REVERSE

Pulling Barton.

FINK
Is Garland Stanford here?

MAITRE D'
He called to say he'd be a few minutes late . . . Ah, here we are . . .

TRACKING IN

Toward a large semi-circular booth. Three guests, two men and a woman in evening wear, are rising and beaming at Barton. A fat middle-aged man, one of the tuxedoed gentlemen we saw backstage, is moving out to let Barton slide in.

MAN

Barton, Barton, so glad you could make it. You know Richard St. Claire . . .

Barton nods and looks at the woman.

. . . and Poppy Carnahan. We're drinking champagne, dear boy, in honor of the occasion. Have you seen the *Herald*?

Barton looks sullenly at his champagne glass as the fat man fills it.

BARTON

Not yet.

MAN

Well, I don't want to embarrass you but Caven could hardly contain himself. But more important, Richard and Poppy here loved the play.

POPPY

Loved it! What power!

RICHARD

Yeah, it was a corker.

BARTON

Thanks, Richard, but I know for a fact the only fish you've ever seen were tacked to the wall of the yacht club.

RICHARD

Ouch!

MAN

Bravo! Nevertheless, we were all devastated.

POPPY

Weeping! Copious tears! What did the *Herald* say?

8

MAN

I happen to have it with me.

BARTON

Please, Derek –

POPPY

Do read it, do!

DEREK

"Bare Ruined Choirs: Triumph of the Common Man. The star of Bare Ruined Choirs was not to be seen on the stage of the Belasco last night – though the thespians involved all acquitted themselves admirably. The find of the evening was the author of this drama about simple folk – fishmongers, in fact – whose brute struggle for existence cannot quite quell their longing for something higher. The playwright finds nobility in the most squalid corners and poetry in the most calloused speech. A tough new voice in the American theater has arrived, and the owner of that voice is named . . . Barton Fink."

BARTON

They'll be wrapping fish in it in the morning so I guess it's not a total waste.

POPPY

Cynic!

DEREK

Well we can enjoy your success, Barton, even if you can't.

BARTON

Don't get me wrong – I'm glad it'll do well for you, Derek.

DEREK

Don't worry about me, dear boy – I want *you* to celebrate.

BARTON

All right, but I can't start listening to the critics, and I can't kid myself about my own work. A writer writes from his gut, and his gut tells him what's good and what's . . . merely adequate.

9

POPPY

Well I don't pretend to be a critic, but Lord, I have a gut, and mine tells me it was simply marvelous.

RICHARD

And a charming gut it is.

POPPY

You dog!

RICHARD
(baying)

Aaa-wooooooo!

Barton turns to look for the source of an insistent jingling. We swish pan off him to find a busboy marching through the restaurant displaying a page sign, bell attached, with Barton's name on it.

TRACKING IN TOWARD A BAR

A distinguished fifty-year-old gentleman in evening clothes is nursing a martini, watching Barton approach.

PULLING BARTON

As he draws near.

BARTON

I thought you were going to join us. Jesus, Garland, you left me alone with those people.

GARLAND

Don't panic, I'll join you in a minute. What'd you think of Richard and Poppy?

Barton scowls.

BARTON

The play was marvelous. She wept, copiously. Millions of dollars and no sense.

Garland smiles, then draws Barton close.

GARLAND
We have to talk a little business. I've just been on the phone to Los Angeles. Barton, Capitol Pictures wants to put you under contract. They've offered you a thousand dollars a week. I think I can get them to go as high as two.

BARTON
To do what?

GARLAND
What do you do for a living?

BARTON
I'm not sure any more. I guess I try to make a difference.

GARLAND
Fair enough. No pressure here, Barton, because I respect you, but let me point out a couple of things. One, here you make a difference to five hundred fifty people a night – *if* the show sells out. Eighty-five million people go to the pictures every week.

BARTON
To see pap.

GARLAND
Yes, generally, to see pap. However, point number two: A brief tenure in Hollywood could support you through the writing of any number of plays.

BARTON
I don't know, Garland; my place is here right now. I feel I'm on the brink of success –

GARLAND
I'd say you're already enjoying some.

Barton leans earnestly forward.

BARTON
No, Garland, don't you see? Not the kind of success where the critics fawn over you or the producers like Derek make a lot of money. No, a real success – the success we've been

dreaming about – the creation of a new, living theater of and about and for the common man! If I ran off to Hollywood now I'd be making money, going to parties, meeting the big shots, sure, but I'd be cutting myself off from the wellspring of that success, from the common man.

He leans back and chuckles ruefully.

. . . I guess I'm spouting off again. But I am certain of this, Garland: I'm capable of more good work. Maybe better work than I did in Choirs. It just doesn't seem to me that Los Angeles is the place to lead the life of the mind.

GARLAND

Okay Barton, you're the artist, I'm just the ten percenter. You decide what you want and I'll make it happen. I'm only asking that your decision be informed by a little realism – if I can use that word and Hollywood in the same breath.

Barton glumly lights a cigarette and gazes out across the floor. Garland studies him.

. . . Look, they love you, kid – everybody does. You see Caven's review in the *Herald*?

BARTON

No, what did it say?

GARLAND

Take my copy. You're the toast of Broadway and you have the opportunity to redeem that for a little cash – strike that, a *lot* of cash.

Garland looks at Barton for a reaction, but gets none.

. . . The common man'll still be here when you get back. What the hell, they might even have one or two of 'em out in Hollywood.

Absently:

BARTON

. . . That's a rationalization, Garland.

Garland smiles gently.

GARLAND

Barton, it was a joke.

We hear a distant rumble. It builds slowly and we cut to:

A GREAT WAVE

Crashing against the Pacific shore.

The roar of the surf slips away as we dissolve to:

HOTEL LOBBY

A high wide shot from the front door, looking down across wilting potted palms, brass cuspidors turning green, ratty wing chairs; the fading decor is deco-gone-to-seed.

Amber light, afternoon turning to evening, slopes in from behind us, washing the derelict lobby with golden highlights.

Barton Fink enters frame from beneath the camera and stops in the middle foreground to look across the lobby.

We are framed on his back, his coat and his hat. The lobby is empty. There is a suspended beat as Barton takes it in.

Barton moves toward the front desk.

THE REVERSE

As Barton stops at the empty desk. He hits a small silver bell next to the register. Its ring-out goes on and on without losing volume.

After a long beat there is the dull scuffle of shoes on stairs. Barton, puzzled, looks around the empty lobby, then down at the floor behind the front desk.

A TRAP DOOR

It swings open and a young man in a faded maroon uniform, holding a shoebrush and a shoe—not one of his own—climbs up from the basement.

He closes the trap door, steps up to the desk and sticks his finger out to touch the small silver bell, finally muting it.

The lobby is now silent again.

> CLERK
>
> Welcome to the Hotel Earle. May I help you, sir?

> BARTON
>
> I'm checking in. Barton Fink.

The clerk flips through cards on the desk.

> CLERK
>
> F-I-N-K. Fink, Barton. That must be you, huh?

> BARTON
>
> Must be.

> CLERK
>
> Okay then, everything seems to be in order. Everything seems to be in order.

He is turning the register around for Barton to sign.

> . . . Are you a tranz or a rez?

> BARTON
>
> Excuse me?

> CLERK
>
> Transient or resident?

> BARTON
>
> I don't know . . . I mean, I'll be here, uh, indefinitely—

> CLERK
>
> Rez. That'll be twenty-five fifty a week payable in advance. Checkout time is twelve sharp only you can forget that on account of you're a rez. If you need anything, anything at all, you dial zero on your personal in-room telephone and talk to me. My name is Chet.

BARTON

Well, I'm going to be working here, mostly at night; I'm a writer. Do you have room service?

CLERK

Kitchen closes at eight but I'm the night clerk. I can always ring out for sandwiches.

The clerk is scribbling something on the back of an index card.

. . . Though we provide privacy for the residential guest, we are also a full service hotel including complimentary shoe shine. My name is Chet.

He pushes a room key across the counter on top of the index card.

Barton looks at the card.

On it: "CHET!"

Barton looks back up at the clerk. They regard each other for a beat.

CLERK

. . . Okay.

BARTON

Huh?

The clerk nods.

CLERK

Okey-dokey, go ahead.

BARTON

What—

CLERK

Don't you wanna go to your room?!

Barton stares at him.

BARTON

. . . What number is it?

The clerk stares back.

CLERK

. . . Six-oh-five. I forgot to tell you.

As Barton stoops to pick up his two small bags:

. . . Those your only bags?

BARTON

The others are being sent.

The clerk leans over the desk to call after him:

CLERK

I'll keep an eye out for them. I'll keep my eyes peeled, Mr. Fink.

Barton is walking to the elevator.

ELEVATOR

Barton enters and sets down his bags.

An aged man with white stubble, wearing a greasy maroon uniform, sits on a stool facing the call panel. He does not acknowledge Barton's presence.

After a beat:

BARTON

. . . Six, please.

The elevator man gets slowly to his feet. As he pushes the door closed:

ELEVATOR MAN

Next stop: Six.

SIXTH-FLOOR HALLWAY

Barton walks slowly toward us, examining the numbers on the doors.

The long, straight hallway is carpeted with an old stained forest green carpet. The wallpaper shows faded yellowing palm trees.

Barton sticks his key in the lock of a door midway down the hall.

16

HIS ROOM

As Barton enters.

The room is small and cheaply furnished. There is a lumpy bed with a worn-yellow coverlet, an old secretary table, and a wooden luggage stand.

As Barton crosses the room we follow to reveal a sink and wash basin, a house telephone on a rickety night stand, and a window with yellowing sheers looking out on an air shaft.

Barton throws his valise onto the bed where it sinks, jittering. He shrugs off his jacket.

Pips of sweat stand out on Barton's brow. The room is hot.

He walks across the room, switches on an oscillating fan and struggles to throw open the window. After he strains at it for a moment, it slides open with a great wrenching sound.

Barton picks up his Underwood and places it on the secretary table. He gives the machine a casually affectionate pat.

Next to the typewriter are a few sheets of the house stationery: THE HOTEL EARLE: A DAY OR A LIFETIME.

We pan up to a picture in a cheap wooden frame on the wall above the desk. A bathing beauty sits on the beach under a cobalt blue sky. One hand shields her eyes from the sun as she looks out at a crashing surf.

The sound of the surf mixes up.

BARTON

Looking at the picture.

TRACKING IN ON THE PICTURE

The surf mixes up louder. We hear a gull cry.

The sound snaps off with the ring of a telephone.

THE HOUSE PHONE

On the nightstand next to the bed. With a groan of bedsprings Barton sits into frame and picks up the telephone.

      VOICE
How d'ya like your room!

      BARTON
. . . Who is this?

      VOICE
Chet!

      BARTON
. . . Who?

      CHET
Chet! From downstairs!

Barton wearily rubs the bridge of his nose.
   . . . How d'ya like your room!

A PILLOW
As Barton's head drops down into frame against it.
He reaches over and turns off the bedside light.
He lies back and closes his eyes.
A long beat.
We hear a faint hum, growing louder.
Barton opens his eyes.

HIS POV

A naked, peeling ceiling.

The hum—a mosquito, perhaps—stops.

BARTON

His eyes move this way and that. After a silent beat, he shuts them again.

After another silent beat we hear—muffled, probably from an adjacent room—a brief dying laugh. It is sighing and weary, like the end of a laughing fit, almost a sob.

Silence again.

We hear the rising mosquito hum.

FADE OUT

EXECUTIVE OFFICE

Barton Fink is ushered into large, light office by an obsequious middle-aged man in a sagging suit.

There are mosquito bites on Barton's face.

REVERSE

From behind a huge white desk a burly man in an expensive suit gets to his feet and strides across the room.

MAN
Is that him?! Is that Barton Fink?! Lemme put my arms around this guy!

He bear-hugs Barton.

. . . How the hell are ya? Good trip?

He separates without waiting for an answer.

My name is Jack Lipnik. I run this dump. You know that—you read the papers.

Lipnik is lumbering back to his desk.

Lou treating you all right? Got everything you need?
What the hell's the matter with your face? What the hell's
the matter with his face, Lou?

BARTON

It's not as bad as it looks; just a mosquito in my room —

LIPNIK

Place okay?

To Lou:

. . . Where did we put him?

BARTON

I'm at the Earle.

LIPNIK

Never heard of it. Let's move him to the Grand, or the
Wilshire, or hell, he can stay at my place.

BARTON

Thanks, but I wanted a place that was less . . .

LIPNIK

Less Hollywood? Sure, say it, it's not a dirty word. Say
whatever the hell you want. The writer is king here at
Capitol Pictures. You don't believe me, take a look at your
paycheck at the end of every week — *that's* what we think of
the writer.

To Lou:

. . . So what kind of pictures does he like?

LOU

Mr. Fink hasn't given a preference, Mr. Lipnik.

LIPNIK

How's about it, Bart?

BARTON

To be honest, I don't go to the pictures much, Mr.
Lipnik —

21

That's okay, that's okay, that's okay – that's just fine. You
probably walked in here thinking that was gonna be a
handicap, thinking we wanted people who knew something
about the medium, maybe even thinking there was all
kinds of technical mumbo-jumbo to learn. You were dead
wrong. We're only interested in one thing: Can you tell a
story, Bart? Can you make us laugh, can you make us cry,
can you make us wanna break out in joyous song? Is that
more than one thing? Okay. The point is, I run this dump
and I don't know the technical mumbo-jumbo. Why do I
run it? I've got horse sense, goddamnit. Showmanship.
And also, and I hope Lou told you this, I'm bigger and
meaner and louder than any other kike in this town. Did
you tell him that, Lou? And I don't mean my dick's bigger
than yours, it's not a sexual thing – although you're the
writer, you would know more about that. Coffee?

BARTON

. . . Yes. Thank you.

LIPNIK

Lou.

*Lou immediately rises and leaves. Lipnik's tone becomes
confidential:*

. . . He used to have shares in the company. An
ownership interest. Got bought out in the twenties –
muscled out according to some. Hell, according to me. So
we keep him around, he's got a family. Poor schmuck.
He's sensitive, don't mention the old days. Oh hell, say
whatever you want. Look, barring a preference, Bart, we're
gonna put you to work on a wrestling picture. Wallace
Beery. I say this because they tell me you know the poetry
of the street. That would rule out westerns, pirate
pictures, screwball, Bible, Roman . . .

He rises and starts pacing.

. . . But look, I'm not one of these guys thinks poetic has
gotta be fruity. We're together on that, aren't we? I mean

22

I'm from New York myself—well, Minsk if you wanna go way back, which we won't if you don't mind and I ain't askin'. Now people're gonna tell you, wrestling, Wallace Beery, it's a B picture. You tell them, bullshit. We don't make B pictures at Capitol. Let's put a stop to *that* rumor right now.

Lou enters with coffee.

   . . . Thanks Lou. Join us. Join us. Talking about the Wallace Beery picture.

LOU

Excellent picture.

LIPNIK

We got a treatment on it yet?

LOU

No, not yet Jack. We just bought the story. *Saturday Evening Post.*

LIPNIK

Okay, the hell with the story. Wallace Beery is a wrestler. I wanna know his hopes, his dreams. Naturally, he'll have to get mixed up with a bad element. And a romantic interest. You know the drill. Romantic interest, or else a young kid. An orphan. What do you think, Lou? Wally a little too old for a romantic interest? Look at me, a writer in the room and I'm askin' Lou what the goddamn story should be!

After a robust laugh, he beams at Barton.

   . . . Well Bart, which is it? Orphan? Dame?

BARTON

   . . . Both, maybe?

There is a disappointed silence. Lipnik looks at Lou.

Lou clears his throat.

LOU

   . . . Maybe we should do a treatment.

23

LIPNIK
Ah, hell, let Bart take a crack at it. He'll get into the
swing of things or I don't know writers. Let's make it a
dame, Bart, keep it simple. We don't gotta tackle the
world our first time out. The important thing is we all
want it to have that Barton Fink feeling. I guess we all
have that Barton Fink feeling, but since you're Barton
Fink I'm assuming you have it in spades. Seriously Bart, I
like you. We're off to a good start. Damnit, if all our
writers were like you I wouldn't have to get so goddamn
involved. I'd like to see something by the end of the week.

Lou is getting to his feet and signaling for Barton to do likewise.

. . . Heard about your show, by the way. My man in
New York saw it. Tells me it was pretty damn powerful.
Pretty damn moving. A little fruity, he said, but I guess
you know what you're doing. Thank you for your heart.
We need more heart in pictures. We're all expecting great
things.

TRACKING SHOT

*We are in the sixth-floor hallway of the Earle, late at night. A
pair of shoes sits before each door. Faintly, from one of the rooms,
we can hear the clack. clack. clack. of a typewriter.*

It grows louder as we track forward.

EXTREME CLOSE SHOT – TYPEWRITER

*Close on the typing so that we see only each letter as it is typed,
without context.*

*One by one the letters clack on: a–u–d–i–b–l–e. After a
short beat, a period strikes.*

BARTON

*Elbows on his desk, he looks down at what he has just written.
He rolls the paper up a few lines, looks some more.*

THE PAGE

It says:

FADE IN

A tenement building on Manhattan's Lower East Side. Early morning traffic is audible.

BARTON

After a beat he rolls the sheet back into place.

EXTREME CLOSE SHOT

The letter-strike area. It is lined up to the last period, which is struck over by a comma. The words "as is" are typed in and we cut back to—

BARTON

—as he continues typing. He stops after several more characters and looks.

Silence.

Breaking the silence, muffled laughter from an adjacent room. A man's laughter. It is weary, solitary, mirthless.

Barton looks up at the wall directly in front of him.

HIS POV

The picture of the girl on the beach.

BARTON

Staring, as the end-of-the-tether laughing continues. Barton looks back down at his typewriter as if to resume work, but the sound is too insistent to ignore.

WIDE SHOT

The room, Barton sitting at his desk, staring at the wall.

The laughter.

Barton pushes his chair back, goes to the door, opens it and looks out.

HIS POV

The empty hallway, a pair of shoes before each door. At the end of the hall a dim red bulb burns over the door to the staircase, punctuating the sick yellow glow of the line of wall sconces.

The laughter, though still faint, is more resonant in the empty hall.

Perhaps because its quality has changed, or perhaps simply because it is so insistent, the laughter now might be taken for weeping.

Barton pauses, trying to interpret the sound. He slowly withdraws into his room.

HIS ROOM

Barton looks down at his typewriter for a beat. The laughter/weeping continues.

He walks over to his bed, sits down and picks up the house phone.

BARTON
Hello, uh . . . Chet? This is Barton Fink in room 605. Yes, there's uh, there's someone in the room next door to mine, 604, and he's uh . . . He's uh . . . making a lot of . . . noise.

After a beat:

. . . Thank you.

He cradles the phone. The laughter continues for a moment or two, then abruptly stops with the muffled sound of the telephone ringing next door.

26

Barton looks at the wall.

The muffled sound of a man talking.

The sound of the earpiece being pronged.

Muffled footsteps next door.

The sound of the neighbor's door opening and shutting.

Footsteps approaching in the hall.

A hard, present knock at Barton's door.

Barton hesitates for a beat, then rises and goes to the door.

ON THE DOOR

As Barton opens it. Standing in the hall is a large man—a very large man—in shirt sleeves, suspenders, and loosened tie. His face is slightly flushed, with the beginnings of a sweat.

MAN
Did you . . . Somebody just complained . . .

Hastily:

BARTON
No, I didn't—I mean, I *did* call down, not to complain exactly, I was just concerned that you might—not that it's my business, but that you might be in some kind of . . . distress. You see, I was trying to work, and it's, well, it was difficult—

MAN
Yeah. I'm damn sorry, if I bothered you. The damn walls here, well, I just apologize like hell . . .

He sticks his hand out.

. . . My name's Charlie Meadows. I guess we're neighbors.

Without reaching for the hand:

BARTON
Barton Fink.

27

Unfazed, Charlie Meadows unpockets a flask.

CHARLIE

Neighbor, I'd feel better about the damned inconvenience
if you'd let me buy you a drink.

BARTON

That's all right, really, thank you.

CHARLIE

All right hell, you trying to work and me carrying on in
there. Look, the liquor's good, wuddya say?

As he enters:

. . . You got a glass? It's the least I can do.

BARTON

Okay . . . a quick one, sure . . .

He gets two glasses from the wash basin.

Charlie sits down on the edge of the bed and uncorks his flask.

CHARLIE

Yeah, just a nip. I feel like a heel, all the carryings-on
next door.

BARTON

That's okay, I assure you. It's just that I was trying to
work —

CHARLIE

What kind of work do you do, Barton, if you don't mind
my asking?

BARTON

Well, I'm a writer, actually.

CHARLIE

You *don't* say. That's a tough racket. My hat's off to
anyone can make a go of it. Damned interesting work, I'd
imagine.

BARTON

Can be. Not easy, but —

29

CHARLIE

Damned difficult, I'd imagine.

As he hands Charlie a glass:

BARTON

And what's your line, Mr. Meadows?

CHARLIE

Hell no! Call me Charlie. Well Barton, you might say I sell peace of mind. Insurance is my game – door-to-door, human contact, still the only way to move the merchandise.

He fills a glass with whiskey and swaps it for the empty glass.

. . . In spite of what you might think from tonight, I'm pretty good at it.

BARTON

Doesn't surprise me at all.

CHARLIE

Hell yes. Because I believe in it. Fire, theft, and casualty are not things that only happen to other people – that's what I tell 'em. Writing doesn't work out, you might want to look into it. Providing for a basic human need – a fella could do worse.

BARTON

Thanks, I'll keep it in mind.

CHARLIE

What kind of scribbler are you – newspaperman did you say?

BARTON

No actually, I'm writing for the pictures now –

CHARLIE

Pictures! Jesus!

He guffaws.

. . . I'm sorry, brother, I was just sitting here thinking I was talking to some ambitious youngster, eager to make

good. Hell, *you've* got it made! Writing for pictures!
Beating out *that* competition! And me being patronizing!

He gestures toward his face:

 . . . Is the egg showing or what?!

                    BARTON
That's okay; actually I *am* just starting out in the
movies – though I was pretty well established in New
York, some renown there.

                    CHARLIE
Oh, it's an exciting time then. I'm not the best-read mug
on the planet, so I guess it's no surprise I didn't recognize
your name. Jesus, I feel like a heel.

For the first time Barton smiles.

                    BARTON
That's okay, Charlie. I'm a playwright. My shows've only
played New York. Last one got a hell of a write-up in the
Herald. I guess that's why they wanted me here.

                    CHARLIE
Hell, why not? Everyone wants quality. What kind of
venue, that is to say, thematically, uh . . .

                    BARTON
What do I write about?

Charlie laughs.

                    CHARLIE
Caught me trying to be fancy! Yeah, that's it, Bart.

                    BARTON
Well, that's a good question. Strange as it may seem,
Charlie, I guess I write about people like you. The average
working stiff. The common man.

                    CHARLIE
Well, ain't that a kick in the head!

BARTON

Yeah, I guess it is. But in a way that's exactly the point. There's a few people in New York—hopefully our numbers are growing—who feel we have an opportunity now to forge something real out of everyday experience, create a theater for the masses that's based on a few simple truths—not on some shopworn abstractions about drama that don't hold true today, if they ever did . . .

He gazes at Charlie.

. . . I don't guess this means much to you.

CHARLIE

Hell, *I* could tell you some stories—

BARTON

And that's the point, that we all have stories. The hopes and dreams of the common man are as noble as those of any king. It's the stuff of life—why shouldn't it be the stuff of theater? Goddamnit, why should that be a hard pill to swallow? Don't call it *new* theater, Charlie; call it *real* theater. Call it *our* theater.

CHARLIE

I can see you feel pretty strongly about it.

BARTON

Well, I don't mean to get up on my high horse, but why shouldn't we look at *ourselves* up there? Who cares about the Fifth Earl of Bastrop and Lady Higginbottom and—and—and who killed Nigel Grinch-Gibbons?

CHARLIE

I can feel my butt getting sore already.

BARTON

Exactly, Charlie! You understand what I'm saying—a lot more than some of these literary types. Because you're a real man!

CHARLIE

And I could tell you some stories—

BARTON

Sure you could! And yet many writers do everything in
their power to insulate themselves from the common
man – from where they live, from where they trade, from
where they fight and love and converse and – and – and
. . . so naturally their work suffers, and regresses into
empty formalism and – well, I'm spouting off again, but to
put it in your language, the theater becomes as phony as a
three-dollar bill.

CHARLIE

Yeah, I guess that's a tragedy right there.

BARTON

Frequently played, seldom remarked.

Charlie laughs.

CHARLIE

Whatever that means.

Barton smiles with him.

BARTON

You're all right, Charlie. I'm glad you stopped by. I'm
sorry if I – well I know sometimes I run on.

CHARLIE

Hell no! Jesus, I'm the kind of guy, I'll let you know if
I'm bored. I find it all pretty damned interesting. I'm the
kind of schmoe who's generally interested in the other
guy's point of view.

BARTON

Well, we've got something in common then.

Charlie is getting to his feet and walking to the door.

CHARLIE

Well Christ, if there's any way I can contribute, or help or
whatever –

Barton chuckles and extends his hand.

BARTON

Sure, sure Charlie, you can help by just being yourself.

CHARLIE

Well, I can tell you some stories.

He pumps Barton's hand, then turns and pauses in the doorway.

. . . And look, I'm sorry as hell about the interruption. Too much revelry late at night, you forget there are other people in the world.

BARTON

See you, Charlie.

Charlie closes the door and is gone.

Barton goes back to his desk and sits.

Muffled, we can hear the door of the adjacent room opening and closing.

Barton looks at the wall.

HIS POV

The bathing beauty.

From offscreen we hear a sticky, adhesive-giving-way sound.

BARTON

He looks around to the opposite — bed — wall.

HIS POV

The wallpaper is lightly sheened with moisture from the heat.

One swath of wallpaper is just finishing sagging away from the wall. About three feet of the wall, where it meets the ceiling, is exposed.

The strip of wallpaper, its glue apparently melted, sags and nods above the bed. It glistens yellow, like a fleshy tropical flower.

34

BACK TO BARTON

*He goes over to the bed and steps up onto it. He smooths the
wallpaper back up against the wall.*

He looks at his hand.

HIS HAND

Sticky with the tacky yellow wall sweat.

He wipes it on his shirt.

We hear a faint mosquito hum.

Barton looks around.

FADE OUT

A TYPEWRITER

*Whirring at high speed. The keys strike too quickly for us to
make out the words.*

SLOW TRACK IN

*On Barton, sitting on a couch in an office anteroom, staring
blankly. Distant phones ring. Barton's eyes are tired and
bloodshot.*

HIS POV

A gargoyle secretary sits typing a document.

*The office door opens in the background and a short middle-aged
man in a dark suit emerges.*

To his secretary:

                    EXECUTIVE
        I'm eating on the lot today—

He notices Barton.

        . . . Who's he?

The secretary looks over from her typing to consult a slip of paper on her desk.

SECRETARY

Barton Fink, Mr. Geisler.

GEISLER

More please.

BARTON

I'm a writer, Mr. Geisler. Ted Okum said I should drop by this morning to see you about the—

GEISLER

Ever act?

BARTON

. . . Huh? No, I'm—

GEISLER

We need Indians for a Norman Steele western.

BARTON

I'm a writer. Ted O—

GEISLER

Think about it, Fink. Writers come and go; we always need Indians.

BARTON

I'm a writer. Ted Okum said you're producing this Wallace Beery picture I'm working on.

GEISLER

What!? Ted Okum doesn't know shit. They've assigned me enough pictures for a goddamn year. What Ted Okum doesn't know you could almost squeeze into the Hollywood Bowl.

BARTON

Then who should I talk to?

Geisler gives a hostile stare. Without looking at her, he addresses the secretary:

36

Get me Lou Breeze.

He perches on the edge of the desk, an open hand out toward the secretary, as he glares wordlessly at Barton.

After a moment:

SECRETARY
Is he in for Mr. Geisler?

She puts the phone in Geisler's hand.

GEISLER
Lou? How's Lipnik's ass smell this morning? . . . Yeah?
. . . Yeah? . . . Yeah? . . . Okay, the reason I'm
calling, I got a writer here, Fink, all screwy. Says I'm
producing that Wallace Beery wrestling picture — what'm I,
the goddamn janitor around here? . . . Yeah, well who'd
you get that from? . . . Yeah, well tell Lipnik he can kiss
my dimpled ass . . . Shit! No, all right . . . No, no, all
right.

Without looking he reaches the phone back. The secretary takes it and cradles it.

:. . . Okay kid, let's chow.

COMMISSARY

Barton and Geisler sit eating in a semicircular booth. Geisler speaks through a mouthful of food:

GEISLER
Don't worry about it. It's just a B picture. I bring it in on
budget, they'll book it without even screening it. Life is
too short.

BARTON
But Lipnik said he wanted to look at the script, see
something by the end of the week.

37

GEISLER

Sure he did. And he forgot about it before your ass left his sofa.

BARTON

Okay. I'm just having trouble getting started. It's funny, I'm blocked up. I feel like I need some kind of indication of . . . what's expected—

GEISLER

Wallace Beery. Wrestling picture. What do you need, a road map?

Geisler chews on his cottage cheese and stares at Barton.

. . . Look, you're confused? You need guidance? Talk to another writer.

BARTON

Who?

Geisler rises and throws his napkin onto his plate.

GEISLER

Jesus, throw a rock in here, you'll hit one. And do me a favor, Fink: Throw it hard.

COMMISSARY MEN'S ROOM

Barton stands at a urinal.

He stares at the wall in front of him as he pees. After a moment, he cocks his head, listening.

We hear throat clearing, as if by a tenor preparing for a difficult passage. It is followed by the gurgling rush of vomit.

Barton buttons his pants and turns to face the stalls.

There is more businesslike throat clearing.

Barton stoops.

HIS POV

We boom down to show the blue serge pants and well-polished shoes of the stall's kneeling occupant.

A white handkerchief has been spread on the floor to protect the trouser knees.

The toilet flushes. The man rises, picks his handkerchief up off the floor and gives it a smart flap.

BARTON

He quickly straightens and goes to the sink. He starts washing his hands. We hear the stall door being unlatched.

Barton glances over his shoulder.

HIS POV

The stall door opening.

BARTON

Quickly, self-consciously, he looks back down at his hands.

HIS POV

His hands writhing under the running water. We hear footsteps approaching.

BARTON

Forcing himself to look at his hands. We hear the man reach the adjacent sink and turn on the tap.

Barton can't help glancing up.

THE MAN

A dapper little man in a neat blue serge suit. He has warm brown eyes, a patrician nose, and a salt-and-pepper mustache. He smiles pleasantly at Barton.

BARTON

He gives a nervous smile — more like a tic — and looks back down at his hands. We hear the man gargling water and spitting into the sink.

After a moment, Barton looks up again.

THE MAN

Reacting to Barton's look as he washes his hands. This time a curt nod accompanies his pleasant smile.

BARTON

Looks back down, then up again.

THE MAN

Extends a dripping hand.

                                MAN
            Bill Mayhew. Sorry about the odor.
His speech is softly accented, from the South.

                              BARTON
            Barton Fink.
They shake, then return to their ablutions.

We hold on Barton as we hear Mayhew's faucet being turned off and his footsteps receding. For some reason, Barton's eyes are widening.

                              BARTON
            . . . Jesus. W. P.!
The dapper little man stops and turns.

                              MAYHEW
            I beg your pardon?

                              BARTON
            W. P. Mayhew? The writer?

40

Just Bill, please.

Barton stands with his back to the sink, facing the little man, his hands dripping onto the floor. There is a short pause. Barton is strangely agitated, his voice halting but urgent.

BARTON

Bill! . . .

Mayhew cocks his head with a politely patient smile. Finally Barton brings out:

. . . You're the finest novelist of our time.

Mayhew leans against a stall.

MAYHEW

Why thank you, son, how kind. Bein' occupied here in the worship of Mammon, I haven't had a chance yet to see your play—

He smiles at Barton's surprise.

. . . Yes, Mistuh Fink, some of the news reaches us in Hollywood.

He is taking out a flask and unscrewing its lid.

BARTON

Sir, I'm flattered that you even recognize my name. My God, I had no idea you were in Hollywood.

MAYHEW

All of us undomesticated writers eventually make our way out here to the Great Salt Lick. Mebbe that's why I allus have such a powerful thust.

He clears his throat, takes a quick swig from the flask, and waves it at Barton.

. . . A little social lubricant, Mistuh Fink?

BARTON

It's still a little early for me.

41

So be it.

He knocks back some more.

BARTON

. . . Bill, if I'm imposing you should say so, I know
you're very busy—I just, uh . . . I just wonder if I could
ask you a favor . . . That is to say, uh . . . have you
ever written a wrestling picture?

Mayhew eyes him appraisingly, and at length clears his throat.

MAYHEW

. . . You are drippin', suh.

*Barton looks down at his hands, then pulls a rough brown paper
towel from a dispenser.*

Mayhew sighs.

. . . Mistuh Fink, they have not invented a genre of
picture that Bill Mayhew has not, at one time or othuh,
been invited to essay. I have taken my stabs at the
wrastlin' form, as I have stabbed at so many others, and
with as little success. I gather that you are a freshman
here, eager for an upperclassman's council. However, just
at the moment . . .

He waves his flask.

. . . I have drinkin' to do. Why don't you stop by my
bungalow, which is numbuh fifteen, later on this
afternoon . . .

He turns to leave.

. . . and we will discuss wrastlin' scenarios and other
things lit'rary.

THE NUMBER "15"

We are close on brass numerals tacked up on a white door.

Muted, from inside, we hear Mayhew's voice—enraged, bellowing.
We hear things breaking. Softer, we hear a woman's voice, its tone
placating.

REVERSE TRACKING SLOWLY IN

on Barton, standing in front of the door.

The noise abates for a moment. We hear the woman's voice
again.

Barton hesitates, listening; he thinks, decides, knocks.

With this the woman's voice stops, and Mayhew starts wailing
again.

The door cracks open.

The woman looks as if she has been crying.

> WOMAN
> . . . Can I help you?

> BARTON
> I'm sorry, I . . . My name is Fink . . . Uh, Bill asked
> me to drop by this afternoon. Is he in?

> WOMAN
> Mr. Mayhew is indisposed at the moment—

From inside the bungalow we hear Mayhew's wail.

> MAYHEW
> HONEY!! WHERE'S M'HONEY!!

The woman glances uncomfortably over her shoulder and steps
outside, closing the door behind her.

> WOMAN
> Mr. Fink, I'm Audrey Taylor, Mr. Mayhew's personal
> secretary. I know this all must sound horrid. I really do
> apologize . . .

Through the door Mayhew is still wailing piteously.

> BARTON
> Is, uh . . . Is he okay?

43

AUDREY
He will be . . . When he can't write, he drinks.

MAYHEW
WHERE ARE YOU, DAMNIT! WHERE'S M'HONEY!!

She brushes a wisp of hair out of her eyes.

AUDREY
I am sorry, it's so embarrassing.

BARTON
How about you? Will you be all right?

AUDREY
I'll be fine . . . Are you a writer, Mr. Fink?

BARTON
Yes, I am. I'm working on a wres — please, call me Barton.

Audrey reaches out and touches Barton's hand.

AUDREY
I'll tell Bill you dropped by. I'm sure he'll want to
reschedule your appointment.

BARTON
Perhaps you and I could get together at some point also.
— I'm sorry if that sounds abrupt. I just . . . I don't know
anyone here in town.

Audrey smiles at him.

AUDREY
Perhaps the three of us, Mr. Fink.

BARTON
Please, Barton.

AUDREY
Barton. You see, Barton, I'm not just Bill's secretary — Bill
and I are . . . in love. We —

MAYHEW'S VOICE
M'HONEY!! WHERE'S M'HONEY!!

*Audrey glances back as we hear the sound of shattering dishes and
heavy footsteps.*

44

                    BARTON
I see.

                    AUDREY
. . . I know this must look . . . funny.

                    BARTON
No, no—

Hurriedly:

                    AUDREY
We need each other. We give each other . . . the things
we need—

                    VOICE
M'HONEY!! . . . bastard-ass sons of bitches . . . the
water's lappin' up . . . M'HONEY!!

                    AUDREY
I'm sorry, Mr. Fink. Please don't judge us. Please . . .

Flustered, she backs away and closes the door.

CLOSE ON A SMALL WRAPPED PACKAGE

Hand-printed on the package is the message:

> Hope these will turn the trick, Mr. Fink.
> —Chet!

The wrapping is torn away and the small box is opened.

Two thumbtacks are taken out.

BARTON'S HOTEL ROOM

*Late at night. The swath of wallpaper behind the bed has sagged
away from the wall again, and has been joined by the swath next
to it.*

Barton enters frame and steps up onto the bed.

*He smooths up the first swath and pushes in a thumbtack near
the top.*

EXTREME CLOSE SHOT

On the tack. As Barton applies pressure to push it in, tacky yellow goo oozes out of the puncture hole and beads around the tack.

ON BARTON

Smoothing up the second swath.

As he pushes in the second tack he pauses, listening.

Muffled, through the wall, we can hear a woman moaning.

After a motionless beat, Barton eases his ear against the wall.

CLOSE ON BARTON

As his ear meets the wall.

The woman's moaning continues. We hear the creaking of bedsprings and her partner, incongruously giggling.

Barton grimaces, gets down off the bed and crosses to the secretary, where he sits. He stares at the paper in the carriage.

HIS POV

The blank part of the page around the key-strike area, under the metal prongs that hold the paper down.

We begin to hear moaning again.

BACK TO BARTON

Still looking; sweating.

HIS POV

Tracking in on the paper, losing the prongs from frame so that we are looking at the pure unblemished white of the page.

The moaning is cut short by two sharp knocks.

THE DOOR

As it swings open.

Charlie Meadows leans in, smiling.

CHARLIE

Howdy, neighbor.

BARTON

Charlie. How are you.

CHARLIE

Jesus, I hope I'm not interrupting you again. I heard you walking around in here. Figured I'd drop by.

BARTON

Yeah, come in Charlie. Hadn't really gotten started yet — what happened to your ear?

—for Charlie's left ear is plugged with cotton wadding. As he enters:

CHARLIE

Oh, yeah. An ear infection, chronic thing. Goes away for a while, but it always comes back. Gotta put cotton in it to staunch the flow of pus. Don't worry, it's not contagious.

BARTON

Seen a doctor?

Charlie gives a dismissive wave.

CHARLIE

Ah, doctors. What's he gonna tell me? Can't trade my head in for a new one.

BARTON

No, I guess you're stuck with the one you got. Have a seat.

Charlie perches on the corner of the bed.

CHARLIE

Thanks. I'd invite you over to my place, but it's a goddamn mess. You married, Bart?

47

BARTON

Nope.

CHARLIE

I myself have yet to be lassoed.

He takes his flask out.

. . . Got a sweetheart?

BARTON

No . . . I guess it's something about my work. I get so worked up over it, I don't know; I don't really have a lot of attention left over, so it would be a little unfair . . .

CHARLIE

Yeah, the ladies do ask for attention. In my experience, they pretend to give it, but it's generally a smoke-screen for demanding it back – with interest. How about family, Bart? How're you fixed in that department?

Barton smiles.

BARTON

My folks live in Brooklyn, with my uncle.

CHARLIE

Mine have passed on. It's just the three of us now . . .

He taps himself on the head, chuckling.

. . . What's the expression – me, myself, and I.

BARTON

Sure, that's tough, but in a sense, we're all alone in the world aren't we, Charlie? I'm often surrounded by family and friends, but . . .

He shrugs.

CHARLIE

Mm . . . You're no stranger to loneliness, then. I guess I got no beef; especially where the dames are concerned. In my line of work I get opportunities galore – always on the wing, you know what I'm saying. I could tell you stories to curl your hair – but it looks like you've already heard 'em!

He laughs at his reference to Barton's curly hair, and pulls a dog-eared photograph from his wallet. As he hands it to Barton:

. . . That's me in Kansas City, plying my trade.

THE PHOTO

Charlie smiles and waves with one foot up on the running board of a 1939 roadster. A battered leather briefcase dangles from one hand.

CHARLIE

. . . It was taken by one of my policy holders. They're more than just customers to me, Barton. They really appreciate what I offer them. Ya see, her hubby was out of town at the time—

BARTON

You know, in a way, I envy you Charlie. Your daily routine—you know what's expected. You know the drill. My job is to plumb the depths, so to speak, dredge something up from inside, something honest. There's no road map for that territory . . .

He looks from Charlie to the Underwood.

. . . and exploring it can be painful. The kind of pain most people don't know anything about.

He looks back at Charlie.

. . . This must be boring you.

CHARLIE

Not at all. It's damned interesting.

BARTON

Yeah . . .

He gives a sad chuckle.

. . . Probably sounds a little grand from someone who's writing a wrestling picture for Wallace Beery.

49

CHARLIE

Beery! You got no beef there! He's good. Hell of an actor – though, for my money, you can't beat Jack Oakie. A stitch, Oakie. Funny stuff, funny stuff. But don't get me wrong – Beery, a wrestling picture, that could be a pip. Wrestled some myself back in school. I guess you know the basic moves.

BARTON

Nope, never even watched any. I'm not that interested in the act itself –

CHARLIE

Okay, but hell, you should know what it is. I can show you the wrestling basics in about thirty seconds.

He is getting down on his hands and knees.

. . . You're a little out of your weight class, but just for the purposes of demonstration –

BARTON

That's all right, really –

CHARLIE

Not a bit of it, compadre! Easiest thing in the world! You just get down on your knees to my left, slap your right hand here . . .

He indicates his own right bicep.

. . . and your left hand here.

He indicates his left bicep.

Barton hesitates.

. . . You can do it, champ!

Barton complies.

. . . All right now, when I say "Ready . . . wrestle!" you try and pin me, and I try and pin you. That's the whole game. Got it?

BARTON

. . . Yeah, okay.

50

Ready . . . wrestle!

With one clean move Charlie flips Barton onto his back, his head and shoulders hitting with a thump. Charlie pins Barton's shoulders with his own upper body.

But before the move even seems completed Charlie is standing again, offering his hand down to Barton.

Damn, there I go again. We're gonna wake the downstairs neighbors. I didn't hurt ya, did I?

Barton seems dazed, but not put out.

BARTON

It's okay, it's okay.

CHARLIE

Well, that's all wrestling is. Except usually there's more grunting and squirming before the pin. Well, it's your first time. And you're out of your weight class.

Barton has propped himself up and is painfully massaging the back of his head. This registers on Charlie.

. . . Jesus, I did hurt you!

He clomps hurriedly away.

. . . I'm just a big, clumsy lug. I sure do apologize.

We hear water running, and Charlie reenters with a wet towel.

Barton accepts the towel and presses it to his head.

. . . You sure you're okay?

Barton gets to his feet.

BARTON

I'm fine, Charlie. Really I am. Actually it's been helpful, but I guess I should get to work.

Charlie looks at him with some concern, then turns and heads for the door.

CHARLIE

Well, it wasn't fair of me to do that. I'm pretty well endowed physically.

He opens the door.

. . . Don't feel bad, though. I wouldn't be much of a match for you at mental gymnastics. Gimme a holler if you need anything.

The door closes.

Barton crosses to the secretary and sits down, rubbing the back of his head. He rolls up the carriage and looks at the page in the typewriter.

HIS POV

The page.

FADE IN

A tenement building on Manhattan's Lower East Side. Early morning traffic is audible, as is the cry of the fishmongers.

BACK TO BARTON

He rubs the back of his head, wincing, as he stares at the page. His gaze drifts up.

HIS POV

The bathing beauty.

BARTON

Looking at the picture. He presses the heels of his hands against his ears.

HIS POV

The bathing beauty. Faint, but building, is the sound of surf.

BARTON

Head cocked. The surf is mixing into another liquid sound. Barton looks sharply around.

THE BATHROOM

Barton enters.

The sink, which Charlie apparently left running when he wet Barton's towel, is overflowing. Water spills onto the tile floor.

Barton hurriedly shuts off the tap, rolls up one sleeve and reaches into the sink.

As his hand emerges, holding something, we hear the unclogged sink gulp water.

53

BARTON'S HAND

Holding a dripping wad of cotton.

BARTON

After a brief, puzzled look he realizes where the cotton came from—and convulsively flips it away.

FADE OUT

FADE IN:

On the title page of a book:

> NEBUCHADNEZZAR
> *By*
> W. P. Mayhew

A hand enters with pen to inscribe:

> To Barton—

> *May this little entertainment divert you in your sojourn among the Philistines.*
>   —Bill

The book is closed and picked up.

WIDER

As—thoomp!—the heavy volume is deposited across the table, in front of Barton, by Mayhew.

Barton, Mayhew, and Audrey are seated around a picnic table. It is one of a few tables littering the lot of a small stucco open-air hamburger stand.

It is peaceful early evening. The last of the sunlight slopes down through palm trees. Barton, Mayhew, and Audrey are the only customers at the stand. Mayhew's black Ford stands alone at the edge of the lot.

Mayhew leans back in his chair.

MAYHEW
If I close m'eyes I can almost smell the live oak.

AUDREY
That's hamburger grease, Bill.

MAYHEW
Well, m'olfactory's turnin' womanish on me – lyin' and deceitful . . .

His eyes still closed, he waves a limp hand gently in the breeze.

. . . Still, I must say. I haven't felt a peace like this since the grand productive days. Don't you find it so, Barton? Ain't writin' peace?

BARTON
Well . . . actually, no Bill . . .

Barton looks nervously at Audrey before continuing.

55

. . . No, I've always found that writing comes from a great inner pain. Maybe it's a pain that comes from a realization that one must do something for one's fellow man—to help somehow to ease his suffering. Maybe it's a personal pain. At any rate, I don't believe good work is possible without it.

MAYHEW

Mmm. Wal, me, I just enjoy makin' things up. Yessir. Escape . . . It's when I can't write, can't escape m'self, that I want to tear m'head off and run screamin' down the street with m'balls in a fruitpicker's pail. Mm . . .

He sighs and reaches for his bottle of Wild Turkey.

. . . This'll sometimes help.

AUDREY

That doesn't help anything, Bill.

BARTON

That's true, Bill. I've never found it to help my writing.

Mayhew is becoming testy:

MAYHEW

Your writing? Son, have you ever heard the story of Solomon's mammy—

Audrey, anticipating, jumps hastily in. She taps the book on the table.

AUDREY

You should read this, Barton. I think it's Bill's finest, or among his finest anyway.

Mayhew looks at her narrowly.

MAYHEW

So now I'm s'posed to roll over like an ol' bitch dog gettin' her belly scratched.

AUDREY

Bill—

56

BARTON

Look, maybe it's none of my business, but a man with
your talent – don't you think your first obligation is to your
gift? Shouldn't you be doing whatever you have to do to
work again?

MAYHEW

And what would that be, son?

BARTON

I don't know exactly. But I do know what you're doing
with that drink. You're cutting yourself off from your gift,
and from Audrey, and from your fellow man, and from
everything your art is about.

MAYHEW

No son, thisahere moonshine's got nothin' to do with
shuttin' folks out. No, I'm usin' it to build somethin'.

BARTON

What's that?

MAYHEW

I'm buildin' a levee. Gulp by gulp, brick by brick. Raisin'
up a levee to keep that ragin' river of manure from lappin'
at m'door.

AUDREY

Maybe you better too, Barton. Before you get buried
under his manure.

Mayhew chuckles.

MAYHEW

M'honey pretends to be impatient with me, Barton, but
she'll put up with anything.

AUDREY

Not anything, Bill. Don't test me.

BARTON

You're lucky she puts up with as much as she does.

Mayhew is getting to his feet.

MAYHEW

Am I? Maybe to a schoolboy's eye. People who know
about the human heart, though, mebbe they'd say, Bill
over here, he gives his honey love, and she pays him back
with pity – the basest coin there is.

AUDREY

Stop it, Bill!

*He wanders over to a corner of the lot between two palm trees,
still clutching his bottle, his back to Barton and Audrey, and
urinates into the grass.*

He is singing – loudly – "Old Black Joe."

Audrey walks over to him.

BARTON

Watching her go.

HIS POV

*Audrey touches Mayhew's elbow. He looks at her, stops singing,
she murmurs something, and he bellows:*

MAYHEW

The truth, m'honey, is a tart that does not bear scrut'ny.

*She touches him again, murmuring, and he lashes out at her,
knocking her to the ground.*

Breach my levee at your peril!

BARTON

He rises.

AUDREY

Coming back to Barton.

MAYHEW

Stumbling off down the dusty road, muttering to himself and waving his bottle of Wild Turkey.

AUDREY

Let him go.

BARTON

That son of a bitch . . . Don't get me wrong, he's a fine writer.

He looks down the road. Mayhew is a small lone figure, weaving in the dust.

MAYHEW

I'll jus' walk on down to the Pacific, and from there I'll . . . improvise.

BARTON

Are you all right?

We hear distant bellowing:

MAYHEW

Silent upon a hill in Darien!

Audrey bursts into tears. Barton puts his arms around her and she leans in to him.

BARTON

Audrey, you can't put up with this.

Gradually she collects herself, wiping her tears.

AUDREY

. . . Oh Barton, I feel so . . . sorry for him!

BARTON

What?! He's a son of a bitch!

AUDREY

No, sometimes he just . . . well, he thinks about Estelle. His wife still lives in Fayettesville. She's . . . disturbed.

BARTON

Really? . . .

He considers this for a moment, but his anger returns.

. . . Well that doesn't excuse his behavior.

                    AUDREY
He'll wander back when he's sober and apologize. He
always does.

                    BARTON
Okay, but that doesn't excuse his—

                    AUDREY
Barton. Empathy requires . . . understanding.

                    BARTON
What. What don't I understand?

Audrey gazes at him.

MAYHEW

*He is very distant now, weaving but somehow dignified in his
light summer suit. "Old Black Joe" floats back to us in the
twilight.*

FADE OUT

BARTON'S HOTEL ROOM

From a high angle, booming down on Barton.

*The room is dark. Barton lies fully clothed, stretched out on the
bed, asleep. The hum of the mosquito fades up in the stillness.*

*Suddenly Barton slaps his cheek. His eyes open, but he remains
still. The hum fades up again.*

*Barton reaches over and turns on the bedside lamp. His eyes shift
this way and that as he waits, listening.*

The hum fades down to silence.

Barton's eyes shift.

HIS POV

The typewriter sits on the secretary, a piece of paper rolled halfway through the carriage.

Barton enters frame and sits down in front of the typewriter.

HIS POV

Next to the typewriter are several crumpled pieces of paper.

The page in the carriage reads:

> FADE IN
>
> *A tenement hotel on the Lower East Side. We can faintly hear the cry of the fishmongers. It is too early for us to hear traffic; later, perhaps, we will.*

BACK TO BARTON

Looking down at the page.

CLOSE ON BARTON'S FEET

Swinging in the legwell.

One foot idly swings over to nudge a pair of nicely shined shoes from where they rest, under the secretary, into the legwell.

We hear typing start.

THE PAGE

A new paragraph being started: "A large man . . . "

BARTON'S FEET

As he slides them into the shoes.

THE PAGE

"A large man in tights . . . "
The typing stops.

BARTON

Looking quizzically at the page. What's wrong?

HIS FEET

Sliding back and forth – swimming – in his shoes, which are several sizes too large.
We hear a knock at the door.

BARTON

He rises and answers the door.
Charlie stands smiling in the doorway, holding a pair of nicely shined shoes.

CHARLIE
I hope these are your shoes.

BARTON
Hi, Charlie.

CHARLIE
Because that would mean they gave you mine.

BARTON
Yeah, as a matter of fact they did. Come on in.

The two stocking-footed men go into the room and Barton reaches under the secretary for Charlie's shoes.

CHARLIE
Jesus, what a day I had. Ever have one of those days?

BARTON
Seems like nothing but, lately.

Charlie perches on the edge of the bed.

CHARLIE

Jesus, what a day. Felt like I couldn't've sold icewater in the Sahara. Jesus. Okay, so you don't want insurance, so okay, that's your loss. But God, people can be rude. Feel like I have to talk to a normal person like you just to restore a little of my . . .

BARTON

Well, my pleasure. I could use a little lift myself.

CHARLIE

A little lift, yeah . . .

Smiling, he takes out his flask.

. . . Good thing they bottle it, huh pal?

He takes a glass from the bedstand and, as he pours Barton a shot:

. . . Did I say rude? People can be goddamn *cruel.* Especially some of these housewives. Okay, so I've got a weight problem. That's my cross to bear. I dunno . . .

63

BARTON

Well it's . . . it's a defense mechanism.

CHARLIE

Defense against what? Insurance? Something they need?
Something they should be thanking me for offering? A
little peace of mind? . . .

He shakes his head.

. . . Finally decided to knock off early, take your advice.
Went to see a doctor about this.

He indicates his ear, still stuffed with cotton.

. . . He told me it was an ear infection. Ten dollars,
please. I said, hell, *I* told *you* my ear was infected. Why
don't *you* give *me* ten dollars? Well, *that* led to an
argument . . .

He gives a rueful chuckle.

. . . Listen to me belly-achin'. As if my problems
amounted to a hill of beans. How goes the life of the
mind?

BARTON

Well, it's been better. I can't seem to get going on this
thing. That one idea, the one that lets you get started – I
still haven't gotten it. Maybe I only had one idea in me –
my play. Maybe once that was done, I was done being a
writer. Christ, I feel like a fraud, sitting here staring at
this paper.

CHARLIE

Those two love-birds next door drivin' you nuts?

Barton looks at him curiously.

BARTON

How do you know about that?

CHARLIE

Know about it? I can practically see how they're doin' it.
Brother, I wish I had a piece of that.

BARTON

Yeah, but—

CHARLIE

Seems like I hear everything that goes on in this dump.
Pipes or somethin'. I'm just glad I don't have to ply *my*
trade in the wee-wee hours.

He laughs.

. . . Ah, you'll lick this picture business, believe me.
You've got a head on your shoulders. What is it they say?
Where there's a head, there's hope.

BARTON

Where there's life there's hope.

Charlie laughs.

CHARLIE

That proves you really are a writer!

Barton smiles.

BARTON

And there's hope for you too, Charlie. Tomorrow I bet
you sell a half-dozen policies.

CHARLIE

Thanks, brother. But the fact is, I gotta pull up stakes
temporarily.

BARTON

You're leaving?

CHARLIE

In a few days. Out to your stompin' grounds as a matter of
fact—New York City. Things have gotten all balled up at
the Head Office.

BARTON

I'm truly sorry to hear that, Charlie. I'll miss you.

CHARLIE

Well hell, buddy, don't pull a long face! This is still home for me – I keep my room, and I'll be back sooner or later . . .

Barton rises and walks over to his writing table.

. . . And – mark my words – by the time I get back you're picture'll be finished, I know it.

Barton scribbles on a notepad and turns to hand it to Charlie.

BARTON

New York can be pretty cruel to strangers, Charlie. If you need a home-cooked meal you just look up Morris and Lillian Fink. They live on Fulton Street with my uncle Dave.

We hear a tacky, tearing sound.

Barton looks toward the door.

Charlie rises and walks over to stand next to where Barton sits.

The two staring men form an odd, motionless tableau – the slight, bespectacled man seated; the big man standing in a hunch with his hands on his thighs; their heads close together.

THEIR POV

A swath of wallpaper in the entryway has pulled away from the wall. It sags and nods.

CHARLIE (*off*)

Christ!

THE TWO MEN

Frozen, looking.

CHARLIE

. . . Your room does that too?

CENTER>BARTON

I guess the heat's sweating off the wallpaper.

CHARLIE

What a dump . . .

He heads for the door and Barton follows.

. . . I guess it seems pathetic to a guy like you.

BARTON

Well . . .

CHARLIE

But it's pathetic, isn't it? I mean to a guy from New York.

BARTON

What do you mean?

CHARLIE

This kind of heat. It's pathetic.

BARTON

Well, I guess you pick your poison.

CHARLIE

So they say.

BARTON

Don't pick up and leave without saying goodbye.

CHARLIE

Course not, compadre. You'll see me again.

Barton closes the door.

He goes back to the desk, sits, and stares at the typewriter. After a beat he tips back in his chair and looks up at the ceiling.

We hear a loud thump.

HIS POV

The ceiling—a white, seamless space.

As we track in the thumping continues—slowly, rhythmically, progressively louder—the effect, it seems, of odd doings upstairs.

LOOKING DOWN ON BARTON

From a high angle, tipped back in his chair, staring at the ceiling.

We track slowly down toward him. The thumping continues, growing louder, sharper.

HIS POV

Moving in on the ceiling. We close in on an unblemished area and cease to have any sense of movement.

With a blur something huge and dark sweeps across the frame to land with a deafening crash, and an instant later it is gone, having left a huge black "T" stamped into the white ceiling.

We are pulling back from the white, past the metal prongs of the key-strike area on a typewriter. More letters appear rapid-fire, growing smaller as the pull back continues. The thumping becomes the clacking of the typewriter.

SWISH PAN

Off the typewriter to track in on Barton.

He is sitting on the sofa in Geisler's outer office. He hasn't shaved. His eyes are bloodshot. He has a mosquito bite on one cheek, daubed with calamine lotion.

The sound of the typing mixes down. We hear a door opening.

BEN GEISLER

is emerging from his office.

As he enters the secretary stops typing, glances down at a slip of paper, and murmurs tonelessly, without looking up:

SECRETARY
Barton Fink.

GEISLER
Yeah. Fink. Come in.

The clack of the typewriter resumes as Barton rises.

GEISLER'S OFFICE

The two men enter.

This office is considerably smaller than Lipnik's, done in grays and black. There are pictures on the wall of Geisler with various celebrities.

Geisler sits behind his desk.

GEISLER

Wuddya got for me—what the hell happened to your face?

BARTON

Nothing. It's just a mosquito bite.

GEISLER

Like hell it is; there are no mosquitos in Los Angeles. Mosquitos breed in swamps—this is a desert town. Wuddya got for me?

BARTON

Well I . . .

GEISLER

On the Beery picture! Where are we? Wuddya got?

BARTON

Well, to tell you the truth, I'm having some trouble getting started—

GEISLER

Getting *started!* Christ Jesus! Started?! You mean you don't have *any*thing?!

BARTON

Well not much.

Geisler leaps to his feet and paces.

GEISLER

What do you think this is? *Hamlet? Gone with the Wind? Ruggles of Red Gap?* It's a goddamn B picture! Big men in tights! You know the drill!

                    BARTON

I'm afraid I don't really understand that genre. Maybe
that's the prob—

                    GEISLER

Understand shit! I thought you were gonna consult
another writer on this!

                    BARTON

Well, I've talked to Bill Mayhew—

                    GEISLER

Bill Mayhew! Some help! The guy's a souse!

                    BARTON

He's a great writer—

                    GEISLER

A souse!

                    BARTON

You don't understand. He's in pain, because he can't
write—

                    GEISLER

Souse! Souse! He manages to write his name on the back
of his paycheck every week!

                    BARTON

But . . . I thought no one cared about this picture.

                    GEISLER

You thought! Where'd you get *that* from? You thought! I
don't know what the hell you said to Lipnik, but the
sonofabitch *likes* you! You understand that, Fink? He *likes*
you! He's taken an interest. *Never* make Lipnik like you!
Never!

Some puzzlement shows through Barton's weariness.

                    BARTON

I don't understand—

                    GEISLER

Are you deaf, he *likes* you! He's taken an interest! What
the hell did you say to him?

70

BARTON

I didn't say anything—

GEISLER

Well he's taken an interest! That means he'll make your life hell, which I could care less about, but since I drew the short straw to supervise this turkey, he's gonna be all over me too! Fat-assed sonofabitch called me yesterday to ask how it's going—don't worry, I covered for you. Told him you were making progress and we were all very excited. I told him it was great, so now *my* ass is on the line. He wants you to tell him all about it tomorrow.

BARTON

I can't write anything by tomorrow.

GEISLER

Who said write? Jesus, Jack can't read. You gotta *tell* it to him—tell him *some*thing for Chrissake.

BARTON

Well what do I tell him?

Geisler rubs a temple, studies Barton for a beat, then picks up the telephone.

GEISLER

Projection . . .

As he waits Geisler gives Barton a withering stare. It continues throughout the phone conversation.

. . . Jerry? Ben Geisler here. Any of the screening rooms free this afternoon? . . . Good, book it for me. A writer named Fink is gonna come in and you're gonna show him wrestling pictures . . . I don't give a shit which ones! *Wrestling* pictures! Wait a minute—isn't Victor Sjoderberg shooting one now? . . . Show him some of the dailies on that.

He slams down the phone.

. . . This ought to give you some ideas.

He jots an address on a piece of paper and hands it to Barton.

71

. . . Eight-fifteen tomorrow morning at Lipnik's house.
Ideas. Broad strokes. Don't cross me, Fink.

SCREEN

*Black-and-white footage. A middle-aged man with a clapstick
enters and shouts:*

CLAPPER
Devil on the Canvas, twelve baker take one.

*Clap! The clapper withdraws. The angle is on a corner of the
ring, where an old cornerman stands behind his charge, a huge
man in tights who is a little too flabby to be a real athlete. His
hair is plastered against his bullet skull and he has a small
mustache.*

VOICE
Action.

*The wrestler rises from his stool and heads toward center ring and
the camera. He affects a German accent:*

WRESTLER
I will destroy him!

He passes the camera.

VOICE
Cut.

Flash frames.

The clapper enters again.

CLAPPER
Twelve baker take two.

Clap! He exits.

The wrestler moves toward the camera.

WRESTLER
I will destroy him!

VOICE
Cut.

The clapper enters.

CLAPPER

Twelve baker take three.

Clap!

WRESTLER

I will destroy him!

SLOW TRACK IN ON BARTON

*Seated alone in the dark screening room, the shaft of the
projection beam flickering over his left shoulder.*

As we creep in closer:

WRESTLER (off)

I will destroy him! . . . I will destroy him! . . . I will
destroy him! . . . I will destroy him!

Another off-microphone, distant voice from the screen:

VOICE

Okay, take five . . .

THE SCREEN

*A jerky pan, interrupted by flash frames. The wrestler is standing
in a corner joking with a makeup girl who pats down his face as
he smokes a cigarette.*

A cut in the film and another clapstick enters.

CLAPPER

Twelve charlie take one—

On the clap:

BACK TO BARTON

Staring at the screen, dull, wan, and forlorn.

VOICE (off)

Action.

73

THE SCREEN

The angle is low – canvas level. We hold for a brief moment on the empty canvas before two wrestlers crash down into frame.

The German is underneath, on his back, pinned by the other man.

The referee enters, cropped at the knees, and throws counting fingers down into frame.

> REFEREE

One . . . two . . .

> WRESTLER

AAAAHHHH!!

The German bucks and throws his opponent off and out of frame.

> VOICE

Cut.

> CLAPPER

Twelve charlie take two.

Crash.

> REFEREE

One . . . two . . .

> WRESTLER

AAAAHHHH!!

BARTON

Glazed.

> WRESTLER (*off*)
AAAAAAHHHHHHH! . . . AAAAAAHHHHHHH!! . . . AAAAAAAAAAAAHHHHHH!!!

PAGE IN TYPEWRITER

The screaming drops out abruptly at the cut. We hear only the sound of heavy footfalls on carpet.

74

Below the opening paragraph, two new words have been added to the typescript:

Orphan?

Dame?

The footfalls continue.

THE HOTEL ROOM

Night. Barton paces frantically back and forth.
He looks at his watch.

HIS POV

It is 12:30.

CLOSE ON THE PHONE

It is lifted out of the cradle.

> BARTON
> Hello, Chet, it's Barton Fink in 605. Can you try a number for me in Hollywood . . . Slausen 6-4304.

We pull back to frame in Barton as we hear his call ring through. Barton sweats.

> Pick it up . . . Pick it up. Pick it—

> AUDREY
> Hello.

> BARTON
> Audrey, listen, I need help. I know it's late and I shouldn't be calling you like this—believe me I wouldn't have if I could see any alternative, but I—I'm sorry—listen, how are you—I'm sorry. You doing okay?

> AUDREY
> . . . Who is this?

75

BARTON

Barton. I'm sorry, it's Barton Fink.

*Through the phone, in the background, we hear Mayhew's
drunken bellowing.*

MAYHEW

Sons of bitches! Drown 'em all!

We hear various objects dropping or being thrown to the floor.

AUDREY

Barton, I'm afraid it's not a good time—

MAYHEW

Drown all those rascals . . .

BARTON

I'm sorry, I just feel like—I know I shouldn't ask, I just
need some kind of help, I just, I have a deadline
tomorrow—

MAYHEW

I said drown 'em all! Who is that?

There is more clatter.

Audrey's voice is hushed, close to the phone:

AUDREY

All right Barton, I'll see if I can slip away—

MAYHEW

Who is that?! Goddamn voices come into the house . . .
sons of bitches . . .

BARTON

If you could, I'd—

AUDREY

If I can. He gets jealous; he—

MAYHEW

Goddamn voices . . . DROWN 'EM!

BARTON

I need help, Audrey.

AUDREY

I'll try to slip out. If he quiets down, passes out . . . I'm afraid he thinks—well, he said you were a buffoon, Barton. He becomes irrational—

MAYHEW

Hesh up! Be still now! DROWN 'EM! DROWN 'EM! DROWN—

WIDE ON THE ROOM

Later. It is quiet. We are craning down toward the bed, where Barton lies stretched out, his head buried beneath a pillow as if to blot out the world.

The track in reveals the wristwatch on Barton's dangling arm: 1:30.

THE HALLWAY

At the end of the dimly lit corridor a red light blinks on over the elevator, with a faint bell.

BACK TO BARTON

With two violent and simultaneous motions he whips the pillow off his head and throws out his other wrist to look at his watch.

There is a knock at the door.

Barton swings his feet off the bed.

THE DOORWAY

Barton opens the door to Audrey.

AUDREY

Hello, Barton.

Audrey, thank you for coming. Thank you. I'm sorry to be
such a . . . such a . . . Thank you.

*They enter the main room, where Audrey perches on the edge of
the bed.*

AUDREY

Now that's all right, Barton. Everything'll be all right.

BARTON

Yes. Thank you. How's Bill?

AUDREY

Oh, he's . . . he drifted off. He'll sleep for a while now.
What is it you have to do, exactly?

Barton paces.

BARTON

Well I have to come up with—an outline, I guess you'd
call it. The story. The whole goddamn story. Soup to
nuts. Three acts. The whole goddamn—

AUDREY

It's all right, Barton. You don't have to write actual
scenes?

BARTON

No, but the whole goddamn—Audrey? Have you ever read
any of Bill's wrestling scenarios?

Audrey laughs.

AUDREY

Yes, I'm afraid I have.

BARTON

What are they like? What are they about?

AUDREY

Well, usually, they're . . . simple morality tales. There's
a good wrestler, and a bad wrestler whom he confronts at
the end. In between the good wrestler has a love interest,
or a small child he has to protect. Bill would usually make
the good wrestler a backwoods type, or a convict. And

78

sometimes, instead of a waif, he'd have the wrestler protecting an idiot manchild. The studio always hated that. Oh, some of the scripts were so . . . spirited!

She laughs—then stops, realizing she has laughed. She looks at Barton.

. . . Barton.

She shakes her head.

. . . Look, it's really just a formula. You don't have to type your soul into it. We'll invent some names and a new setting. I'll help you and it won't take any time at all. I did it for Bill so many times—

Barton's pacing comes up short.

> BARTON
> Did what for Bill?

Guardedly:

> AUDREY
> Well . . . *this.*

> BARTON
> You wrote his scripts for him?

> AUDREY
> Well . . . the basic ideas were frequently his—

> BARTON
> You wrote Bill's scripts! Jesus Christ, you wrote his—what about before that?

> AUDREY
> Before what?

> BARTON
> Before Bill came to Hollywood.

Audrey is clearly reluctant to travel this path.

> AUDREY
> Well, Bill was *always* the author, so to speak—

BARTON
What do you mean so to speak?! Audrey, how long have
you been his . . . secretary?

AUDREY
Barton, I think we should concentrate on *our* little
project —

BARTON
I want to know how many of Bill's books you wrote!

AUDREY
Barton!

BARTON
I want to know!

AUDREY
Barton, honestly, only the last couple —

BARTON
Hah!

AUDREY
And my input was mostly . . . *editorial*, really, when he'd
been drinking —

BARTON
I'll bet. Jesus — "The grand productive days." What a
goddamn phony.

He resumes pacing.

. . . W. P. Mayhew. William Goddamn Phony Mayhew.
All his guff about escape. Hah! *I'll* say he escaped!

Barton sighs and looks at his watch.

. . . Well, we don't have much time.

He sits down next to Audrey. Audrey's tone is gentle:

AUDREY
It'll be fine . . . Don't judge him, Barton. Don't
condescend to him . . .

She strokes Barton's hair.

. . . It's not as simple as you think. I helped Bill most by appreciating him, by understanding him. We all need understanding, Barton. Even you, tonight, it's all you really need . . .

She kisses him.

As Barton tentatively responds, we are panning away.

We frame up on the door to the bathroom and track in toward the sink. We can hear the creak of bedsprings and Audrey and Barton's breath, becoming labored.

The continuing track brings us up to and over the lip of the sink to frame up its drain, a perfect black circle in the porcelain white.

We track up to the drain and are enveloped by it as the sound of lovemaking mixes into the groaning of pipes.

BLACK

FADE IN

BARTON

The hum of a mosquito brings us out of the black and we are looking down at Barton, in bed, asleep. It is dawn.

Barton's eyes snap open.

HIS POV

The white ceiling. A humming black speck flits across the white.

BARTON

Slowly, cautiously, he props himself up, his look following the sound of the mosquito.

His gaze travels down and to one side and is arrested as the hum stops.

HIS POV

Audrey lies facing away on her side of the bed, half-covered by a blanket.

BARTON

Gingerly, he reaches over and draws the blanket down Audrey's back.

HIS POV

The alabaster white of Audrey's back.

The mosquito is feeding on it.

EXTREME CLOSE ON BARTON'S EYES

Looking.

EXTREME CLOSE ON THE MOSQUITO
Swelling with blood.

WIDER

*As Barton's hand comes through frame and slaps Audrey's back.
She doesn't react.*
*Barton draws his hand away. Audrey's back is smeared with
blood.*

ON BARTON
He looks at his hand

HIS POV
His hand is dripping with blood. Too much blood.

BACK TO BARTON
Eyes wide, he looks down at the bed.

HIS POV
Blood seeps up into the sheet beneath the curve of Audrey's back.

BARTON
He pulls Audrey's shoulder.

AUDREY
She rolls onto her back. Her eyes are wide and lifeless.
*Her stomach is nothing but blood. The top sheet, drawn to her
waist, is drenched red and clings to her body.*

BARTON

He screams.

He screams again.

We hear rapid and heavy footfalls next door, a door opening and closing, and then loud banging on Barton's door.

Barton's head spins toward the door. He is momentarily frozen.

Another knock.

Barton leaps to his feet and hurries to the door.

THE DOORWAY

Over Barton's shoulder as he cracks the door.

Charlie stands in the hall in his boxer shorts and a sleeveless tee.

                    CHARLIE
    Are you all right?

Barton stares dumbly for a moment.

    . . . Can I come in?

                    BARTON
    No! . . . I'm fine. Thank you.

                    CHARLIE
    Are you sure—

                    BARTON
    No . . . no . . .

Barton is nodding as he shuts the door in Charlie's face.

He walks back into the room.

HIS POV

Audrey's corpse, in long shot, face up on the bed.

BARTON

He walks toward the bed, wheels before he reaches it, and starts back toward the door.

He stops short and turns back again to the room. He averts his eyes — as it happens, toward the secretary.

He walks stiffly over and sits, his back to Audrey.

CLOSE ON BARTON

As he sits in. He stares emptily down at the desk, in shock, totally shut down. Behind him, we can see Audrey on the bed.

He stares for a long beat.

Strange, involuntary respiratory noises come from his throat. He is not in control.

Becoming aware of the noise he is making, he stops.

He lurches to his feet.

THE DOORWAY

As Barton enters, opens the door, and sticks his head out.

HALLWAY

Barton peers out to see if the coast is clear.

HIS POV

The long hallway.

In the deep background, Chet, the night clerk, is stooping in front of a door to pick up a pair of shoes. Next to him is a castored shoe caddy.

All of the doorways between us and Chet are empty of shoes.

CHET

Close on him as, mid-stoop, he looks up.

CHET'S POV

Up the long hall. In the deep background a door is closing.

CHET

He pauses, then straightens up and puts the shoes on the shoe caddy. It squeaks as he pushes it on down the hall.

BARTON'S ROOM

Barton stands at the door, listening to a very faint squeak. Eventually it becomes inaudible.

He cracks the door again, looks out, and exits.

HALLWAY

Barton goes to Charlie's door and knocks.

Footfalls end as the door is cracked open.

                    CHARLIE
        Barton. Are you all right?
                    BARTON
        No . . . Can I come in?
                    CHARLIE
        Why don't we go to your room—
                    BARTON
        Charlie, I'm in trouble. You've gotta help me.

Once again he is breathing hard.

Charlie steps out into the hall and shuts the door behind him.

CHARLIE

Get a grip on yourself, brother. Whatever the problem is, we'll sort it out.

BARTON

Charlie, I'm in trouble – something horrible's happened – I've gotta call the police . . .

Charlie leads him toward his room.

. . . Will you stay with me till they get here?

CHARLIE

Don't worry about it, Barton. We can sort it –

He is pushing Barton's door open, but Barton grabs an elbow to stop him.

BARTON

Before you go in – I didn't do this. I don't know how it happened, but I didn't . . . I want you to know that . . .

Charlie looks into his eyes. For a moment the two men stare at each other – Charlie's look inquisitive, Barton's supplicating.

Finally, Charlie nods.

CHARLIE

Okay.

He turns and pushes open the door.

BARTON'S ROOM

The two men enter.

Barton lingers by the door. Charlie walks into the foreground to look off toward the bed.

His eyes widen and he screams.

He turns and disappears into the bathroom. We hear vomiting, then the flush of the toilet.

CHARLIE

Jesus . . . Jesus . . . Jesus have mercy . . .

His reaction has not encouraged Barton, who is more and more agitated.

Charlie emerges from the bathroom, sweating.

. . . Jesus, Barton, what the hell is this? What're we gonna do?

BARTON

I've gotta call the police – or you could call for me –

CHARLIE

Hold on –

BARTON

You gotta believe me –

CHARLIE

Hold on –

BARTON

I didn't do this, I did *not* do this –

CHARLIE

Hold on. Stop. Take a deep breath. Tell me what happened.

BARTON

I don't know! I woke up, she was . . . God, you gotta believe me!

Charlie, in spite of himself, is sneaking horrified glances back into the room.

CHARLIE

I believe you, brother, but this don't look good.

BARTON

We gotta call the police –

CHARLIE

Hold on. I said hold on, so hold on.

BARTON

Yeah.

CHARLIE

What do you think happened?

88

BARTON

I don't know! Maybe it was her . . . boyfriend. I passed
out. I don't know. Won't the police be able to—

CHARLIE

Stop with the police! Wake up, friend! This does not look
good! They hang people for this!

BARTON

But I didn't do it—don't you believe me?

CHARLIE

I believe you—I *know* you. But why should the police?

Barton gives him a dumb stare.

. . . Did you . . . Barton, between you and me, did you
have sexual intercourse?

Barton stares at Charlie. He swallows.

Charlie shakes his head.

Jesus . . . They can tell that . . .

BARTON

They *gotta* believe me, Charlie! They gotta have mercy!

CHARLIE

You're in pictures, Barton. Even if you got cleared
eventually, this would ruin you.

He turns and starts toward the bed.

. . . Wait in the bathroom.

BATHROOM

*Later. Barton, still in his underwear, sits leaning against the
wall, staring glassily at his feet.*

*From the other room we hear the creak of bedsprings and the
sound of the bed clothes being torn off.*

*Finally there is a last creak of bedsprings and the sound of
Charlie grunting under great weight.*

We hear heavy footsteps approaching.

Barton looks up through the open bathroom door.

HIS POV

Charlie is groping for the front doorknob, cradling the sheet-swaddled body in his arms.

BACK TO BARTON

His neck goes rubbery. His eyes roll up. His heads lolls back to hit the wall.

BLACK

Slap! Slap!

We are low on Charlie, who is following through on a slap and backing away, having roused Barton. Charlie is now wearing pants but is still in his sleeveless tee, which has blood flecks across the belly.

> CHARLIE

You passed out.

Barton looks groggily up.

> BARTON

. . . Uh-huh . . . Where's Audrey?

> CHARLIE

She's dead, Barton! She's dead! If that was her name.

TRACKING IN ON BARTON

He stares at Charlie.

> CHARLIE (*off*)

Barton, listen to me. You gotta act as if nothing's happened. Put this totally out of your head. I know that's hard, but your play from here on out is just to go on about your business as usual. Give us some time to sort this out . . .

90

Barton looks at his watch.

THE WATCH

7:45.

> CHARLIE (*off*)
> . . . Just put it out of your head . . .

TRACKING

Toward a pool set in a grand yard with shaped hedges and statuary set amid palm trees.

Sunlight glitters angrily off the water; we are approaching Jack Lipnik who sits poolside in a white deck chair.

> LIPNIK
> Bart! So happy to see ya!

REVERSE

Pulling Barton, who is being escorted by Lou Breeze.

Barton is haggard, sunken eyes squinting against too much sun.

> LIPNIK
> Sit! Talk! Relax for a minute, then talk! Drink?

As Barton sits:

> BARTON
> Yeah . . . rye whiskey?

> LIPNIK
> Boy! You writers! Work hard, play hard! That's what I hear, anyway . . .

He laughs, then barks at Lou Breeze.

> . . . Lou.

Lou exits.

LIPNIK

Anyway. Ben Geisler tells me things're going along great. Thinks we've got a real winner in this one. And let me tell you something, I'm counting on it. I've taken an interest. Not to interfere, mind you – hardly seems necessary in your case. A writer – a storyteller – of your stature. Givitta me in bold strokes, Bart. Gimme the broad outlines. I'm sitting in the audience, the lights go down, Capitol logo comes up . . . you're on!

He beams expectantly at Barton.

Barton licks his parched lips.

BARTON

Yeah, okay . . . well . . . we fade in . . .

Lipnik is nodding, already involved in the story.

. . . It's a tenement building. On the Lower East Side . . .

LIPNIK

Great! He's poor, this wrestler! He's had to struggle!

BARTON

And then . . . well . . .

Barton looks out at the pool, his eyes closed to slits against the sun. He looks back at Lipnik.

. . . Can I be honest, Mr. Lipnik?

LIPNIK

Can you? You damn well better be. Jesus, if I hadn't been honest in my business dealings – well of course, you can't always be honest, not with the sharks swimming around this town – but you're a writer, you don't think about those things – if I'd been totally honest, I wouldn't be within a mile of this pool – unless I was cleaning it. But that's no reason for you not to be. Honest, I mean. Not cleaning the pool.

Lou has entered with a drink, which he sets next to Barton. Lou sits.

Barton looks around, takes the drink, sips at it greedily, but must finally take the plunge.

BARTON

Well . . . to be honest, I'm never really comfortable discussing a work in progress. I've got it all worked out in my head, but sometimes if you force it into words—prematurely—the wrong words—well, your meaning changes, and it changes in your own mind, and you never get it back—so I'd just as soon not talk about it.

Lipnik stares at him. His smile has disappeared. There is a long beat.

Lou Breeze clears his throat. He apparently feels obliged to fill the silence.

LOU

. . . Mr. Fink. Never mind me. Never mind how long I've been in pictures. Mr. Lipnik has been in pictures just about since they were invented. *He* practically invented them.

Lipnik has turned to look curiously at Lou.

. . . Now I think if he's interested in what one of his contract employees is doing while he draws pay, I think that employee ought to tell him, if he wants to stay an employee. Right now the contents of your head are the property of Capitol Pictures, so if I were you I would speak up. And pretty goddamn fast.

Lou looks at Barton, expectantly. Lipnik continues to stare at Lou.

There is a long silence, terribly heavy.

Finally Lipnik explodes—at Lou:

LIPNIK

You lousy kike sonofabitch! You're telling this man—this *artist*—what to do?!

Lou Breeze is stunned.

93

LOU

Mr. Lipnik, I –

LIPNIK

This man creates for a living! He puts the food on your table and on mine! *Thank* him for it! Thank him, you ungrateful sonofabitch! Thank him or *you're* fired!

Barton is staring, aghast.

BARTON

Mr. Lipnik, that's really not necessar –

Lipnik, still staring at Lou, gives no sign of hearing Barton. He rises and points.

LIPNIK

Get down on your knees, you sonofabitch! Get down on your knees and kiss this man's feet!

LOU

Mr. Lipnik, please –

BARTON

I – Mr. Lipnik –

LIPNIK

KISS THIS MAN'S FEET!

Lou, aghast, looks at Barton.

Barton, aghast, can only return the same stunned look.

Lipnik snarls at Lou:

. . . Okay, get out of here. You're fired, you understand me? Get out of my sight.

Lou gets stiffly to his feet and stumbles away.

BARTON

Mr. Lipnik, I –

LIPNIK

I apologize, Barton.

BARTON

No no, Mr. Breeze has actually been a great help –

94

LIPNIK

You don't have to cover for him. It's noble of you, but
these things happen in business.

BARTON

Mr. Lipnik, I really would feel much better if you could
reconsider —

LIPNIK

Ah, forget it, kid. I want you to put this out of your head.
If that sonofabitch wouldn't apologize to you, goddamnit, I
will. I respect your artistry and your methods, and if you
can't fill us in yet, well hell, we should be kissing your
feet for your fine efforts.

He gets down on his knees in front of Barton.

. . . You know in the old country we were taught, as very
young children, that there's no shame in supplicatin'
yourself when you respect someone.

Barton stares, horrified, at Lipnik, on the ground at his feet.

. . . On behalf of Capitol Pictures, the administration,
and all a the stockholders, please accept this as a symbol
of our apology and respect.

BARTON'S POV

Lipnik kisses his shoe and looks up at him.

Behind Lipnik the pool glitters.

BARTON'S ROOM

*The cut has a hard musical sting. Out of the sting comes a loud
but distorted thumping noise.*

*We are looking down, high angle, from one corner of the room.
We are presented with a motionless tableau: Barton sits, hunched,
in the far corner, elbows on knees, staring at the bed in front of
him. He wears only trousers and a T-shirt and his body and face*

95

glisten with sweat. The bed's sheets have been stripped and the ratty gray mattress has an enormous rust-red stain in the middle.

After a beat, in the foreground, the only motion in the scene: A bead of tacky yellow wall-sweat dribbles down the near wall.

Silence, then the thumping repeats, resolving itself into a knock at the door.

Barton rises slowly and crosses to the door.

THE DOOR

Barton opens it to Charlie, who is dressed in a baggy suit, his hair slicked back, a tan fedora pushed back on his head. It is the first time we have seen him well turned out.

A battered briefcase is on the floor next to him. He holds a parcel in his left hand, about one foot square, wrapped in brown paper and tied up with twine.

CHARLIE

Barton. Can I come in?

Barton stands back from the door and Charlie picks up his briefcase and enters.

THE ROOM

As the two men enter.

BARTON

Jesus . . . You're leaving.

CHARLIE

Have to, old timer. Just for a while.

Barton sounds desperate:

BARTON

Jesus, Charlie, I . . .

CHARLIE

Everything's okay, believe me. I know it's rough mentally, but everything's taken care of.

BARTON

Charlie! I've got no one else here! You're the only person I know in Los Angeles . . .

He starts weeping.

. . . that I can talk to.

Charlie, also disturbed and unhappy, wraps both arms around Barton.

Barton sobs unashamed into his shoulder. Charlie is somber.

CHARLIE

It's okay . . . It's okay . . .

BARTON

Charlie, I feel like I'm going crazy—like I'm losing my mind. I don't know what to do . . . I didn't do it, believe me. I'm sure of that, Charlie. I just . . .

His breath comes in short gasping heaves.

. . . I just don't know what . . . to do—

CHARLIE

You gotta get a grip on, brother. You gotta just carry on—just for a few days, till I get back. Try and stay here, keep your door locked. Don't talk to anyone. We just gotta keep our heads and we'll figure it out.

BARTON

Yeah, but Charlie—

CHARLIE

Damnit, don't argue with me. You asked me to believe you—well I do. Now don't argue with me.

He looks at Barton for a beat.

. . . Look, pal—can you do something for me?

Charlie hands him his parcel.

. . . Keep this for me, till I get back.

Barton, snuffling, accepts the package.

97

. . . It's just personal stuff. I don't wanna drag it with
me, but I don't trust 'em downstairs, and I'd like to think
it's in good hands.

Still snuffling:

> ### BARTON
> Sure, Charlie.

> ### CHARLIE
> Funny, huh, when everything that's important to a guy,
> everything he wants to keep from a lifetime – when he can
> fit it into a little box like that. I guess . . . I guess it's
> kind of pathetic.

Wallowing in self-pity:

> ### BARTON
> It's more than I've got.

> ### CHARLIE
> Well, keep it for me. Maybe it'll bring you good luck.
> Yeah, it'll help you finish your script. You'll think about
> me . . .

He thumps his chest.

> . . . Make me your wrestler. Then you'll lick that story
> of yours.

Barton is tearfully sincere:

> ### BARTON
> Thanks, Charlie.

Charlie solemnly thrusts out his hand.

> ### CHARLIE
> Yeah, well, see you soon, friend. You're gonna be fine.

Barton shakes. As they walk to the door:

> ### BARTON
> You'll be back?

> ### CHARLIE
> Don't worry about that, compadre. I'll be back.

Barton shuts the door behind Charlie, locks it, and turns around.

HIS POV

The room. The bed. The blood-stained mattress.

Barton walks across the room and sits carefully on the edge of the bed, avoiding the rust-colored stain. For a long beat he sits still, but something is building inside.

Finally, when we hear the distant ding of the elevator arriving for Charlie, it erupts:

Barton sobs, with the unself-conscious grief of an abandoned child.

HIGH WIDE SHOT

Barton weeping, alone on the bed, next to the rust-colored stain.

FADE OUT

FADE IN
BATHING BEAUTY

With the fade in the sound of the surf mixes up.

We pan down the picture to discover that a snapshot has been tucked into a corner of the picture frame: it is the snap of Charlie, smiling and waving, with his foot up on the running board of the 1939 Ford roadster.

BARTON

Sitting at the desk, staring at the picture. From his glazed eyes and the way his mouth hangs open, we may assume he has been staring at the picture for some time.

He notices something on the desk and picks it up.

HIS POV

The Holy Bible – Placed by the Gideons.

99

Barton opens it, randomly, to the Book of Daniel. The text is set in ornately Gothic type:

> 5. *And the king, Nebuchadnezzar, answered and said to the Chaldeans, I recall not my dream; if ye will not make known unto me my dream, and its interpretation, ye shall be cut in pieces, and of your tents shall be made a dunghill.*

BARTON

Staring at the passage. His mouth hangs open.

THE BIBLE

Barton riffles through to the first page.

In bold type at the top:

> THE BOOK OF GENESIS

Underneath, in the same ornate Gothic type:

> Chapter One
> 1. *Fade in on a tenement building on Manhattan's Lower East Side. Faint traffic noise is audible;*
> 2. *As is the cry of the fishmongers.*

BARTON

Squinting at the page through bloodshot eyes.

His mouth hangs open.

BARTON'S ROOM – DAY

At the cut the harsh clackety-clack of typing bangs in. Sunlight burns against the sheers of Barton's window, making it a painfully bright patch in the room which itself remains fairly dim.

Barton sits at the secretary, typing furiously.

He finishes a page, yanks it out of the carriage, and places it face-down on a short stack of face-down pages.

He feeds in a blank sheet and resumes his rapid typing. He is sweating, unshaven, and more haggard even than when we left him the previous night.

The telephone rings. After several rings Barton stops typing and answers it, absently, still looking at his work. His voice is hoarse.

BARTON

Hello . . . Chet . . . Who? . . .

He puts the receiver down on the desk, leans over the typewriter, and examines something he has just written.

He picks the phone back up and listens for a beat.

. . . No, don't send them up here. I'll be right down.

ELEVATOR

A small oscillating fan whirs up in a corner of the elevator.

We pan down to Barton, who is riding down with Pete, the old elevator operator. Barton's voice is hoarse with fatigue:

BARTON

. . . You read the Bible, Pete?

PETE

Holy Bible?

BARTON

Yeah.

PETE

I think so . . . Anyway, I've heard about it.

Barton nods.

They ride for a beat.

LOBBY

Late afternoon sun slants in from one side. The lobby has the same golden ambiance as when first we saw it.

Barton is walking toward two wing chairs in the shadows, from which two men in suits are rising. One is tall, the other short.

Fink?

Yeah.

POLICEMAN 2
Detective Mastrionotti.

POLICEMAN I
Detective Deutsch.

MASTRIONOTTI
L.A.P.D.

BARTON
Uh-huh.

All three sit in ancient maroon wing chairs. Mastrionotti perches on the edge of his chair; Deutsch slumps back in the shadows, studying Barton.

DEUTSCH
Got a couple questions to ask ya.

MASTRIONOTTI
What do you do, Fink?

Still hoarse:

BARTON
I write.

DEUTSCH
Oh yeah? What kind of write?

BARTON
Well, as a matter of fact, I write for the pictures.

MASTRIONOTTI
Big fuckin' deal.

DEUTSCH
You want my partner to kiss your ass?

MASTRIONOTTI
Would that be good enough for ya?

BARTON

No, I—I didn't mean to sound—

DEUTSCH

What *did* you mean?

BARTON

I—I've got respect for—for working guys, like you—

MASTRIONOTTI

Jesus! Ain't *that* a load off! You live in 605?

BARTON

Yeah.

DEUTSCH

How long you been up there, Fink?

BARTON

A week, eight, nine days—

MASTRIONOTTI

Is this multiple choice?

BARTON

Nine days—Tuesday—

DEUTSCH

You know this slob?

He is holding a small black-and-white photograph out toward Barton.

There is a long beat as Barton studies the picture.

BARTON

. . . Yeah, he . . . he lives next door to me.

MASTRIONOTTI

That's right, Fink, he lives next door to you.

DEUTSCH

Ever talk to him?

BARTON

. . . Once or twice. His name is Charlie Meadows.

MASTRIONOTTI
Yeah, and I'm Buck Rogers.

DEUTSCH
His name is Mundt. Karl Mundt.

MASTRIONOTTI
Also known as Madman Mundt.

DEUTSCH
He's a little funny in the head.

BARTON
What did . . . What did he –

MASTRIONOTTI
Funny. As in, he likes to ventilate people with a shotgun
and then cut their heads off.

DEUTSCH
Yeah, he's funny that way.

BARTON
I . . .

MASTRIONOTTI
Started in Kansas City. Couple of housewives.

DEUTSCH
Couple days ago we see the same M.O. out in Los Feliz.

MASTRIONOTTI
Doctor. Ear, nose and throat man.

DEUTSCH
All of which he's now missin'.

MASTRIONOTTI
Well, some of his throat was there.

DEUTSCH
Physician, heal thyself.

MASTRIONOTTI
Good luck with no fuckin' head.

DEUTSCH
Anyway.

MASTRIONOTTI

Hollywood precinct finds another stiff yesterday. Not too far from here. This one's better looking than the doc.

DEUTSCH

Female caucasian, thirty years old. Nice tits. No head. You ever see Mundt with anyone meets that description?

MASTRIONOTTI

But, you know, with the head still on.

BARTON

. . . No. I never saw him with anyone else.

DEUTSCH

So. You talked to Mundt, what about?

BARTON

Nothing, really. Said he was in the insurance business.

Deutsch indicates Mastrionotti.

DEUTSCH

Yeah, and he's Buck Rogers.

MASTRIONOTTI

No reputable company would hire a guy like that.

BARTON

Well that's what he said.

DEUTSCH

What else?

BARTON

He . . . I'm trying to think . . . Nothing, really . . . He . . . He said he liked Jack Oakie pictures.

Mastrionotti looks at Deutsch. Deutsch looks at Mastrionotti. After a beat, Mastrionotti looks back at Barton.

MASTRIONOTTI

Ya know, Fink, ordinarily we say anything you might remember could be helpful. But I'll be frank with you: That is not helpful.

DEUTSCH
Ya see how he's not writing it down?

MASTRIONOTTI
Fink. That's a Jewish name, isn't it?

BARTON
Yeah.

Mastrionotti gets to his feet, looking around the lobby.

MASTRIONOTTI
Yeah, I didn't think this dump was restricted.

He digs in his pocket.

. . . Mundt has disappeared. I don't think he'll be back.
But . . .

He hands Barton a card.

. . . give me a call if you see him. Or if you remember
something that isn't totally idiotic.

BARTON'S ROOM

*We are tracking toward the paper-wrapped parcel that sits on the
nightstand next to Barton's bed.*

*Barton enters and picks it up. He holds it for a beat, looking at
it, then brings it over to the secretary and sits.*

He shakes it.

No sound; whatever is inside is well packed.

*Barton holds it up to his ear and listens for a long beat, as if it
were a seashell and he is listening for the surf.*

*Finally he puts it on the desk, beneath the picture of the bathing
beauty, and starts typing, quickly and steadily.*

DISSOLVE THROUGH TO:
REVERSE

*Some time later; Barton still types. He is face to us; beyond him
we can see the bed with its rust-colored stain.*

106

The phone rings. Barton ignores it. It continues to ring.

Barton rises and exits frame; we hold on the bed in the background. We hear Barton's footsteps on the bathroom tile as the phone continues ringing.

Barton sits back into frame stuffing cotton wadding into each ear. He resumes typing.

ANOTHER ANGLE

Barton typing. The desk trembles under the working of the typewriter. Charlie's parcel chatters.

Barton takes a finished page out of the carriage and places it face down on the growing stack to his right. He feeds in a new page. We hear the muted ding of the elevator down the hall. Barton resumes typing.

We hear a knock at Barton's door. Barton does not react, apparently not hearing. He continues to type.

THE DOORWAY

We are close on the bottom of the door. Someone in the hallway is sliding a note beneath the door; then his shadow disappears and his footsteps recede.

The note is a printed message form headed: "While You Were Out . . . " Underneath are printed the words: "You were called by" and, handwritten in the space following: "Mr. Ben Geisler."

Handwritten below, in the message space:

> *Thank you.*
> *Lipnik loved your meeting.*
> *Keep up the good work.*

Barton's offscreen typing continues steadily.

FADE OUT

HALLWAY

A perfectly symmetrical wide low angle shot of the empty hall. Shoes are set out in front of each door except for one in the middle background.

At the cut in we hear faint, regular typing.

We hold for a long beat. There is no motion. The long, empty hall. The distant typing.

We hold.

The typing stops. There is a beat of quiet.

It is broken by the sound of a door opening. It is the shoeless door in the middle background.

A hand reaches out to place a pair of shoes in the hallway.

The hand withdraws.

The door closes.

A short beat of silence.

The distant typing resumes.

The long empty hall. The distant typing.

FADE OUT

Over black we hear the distant sound of a woman's voice, tinny and indistinct:

> WOMAN
> Just a minute and I'll connect you . . .

FADE IN
CLOSE ON BARTON

His eyes are red-rimmed and wild. He sits on the edge of his bed holding the phone to his ear.

His voice is unnaturally loud:

> BARTON
> Hello? Operator! I can't . . . Oh!

He stops, reaches up, takes a cotton wad out of his ear.

We hear various clicks and clacks as the telephone lines switch, and then a distant ring. The phone rings three or four times before it is answered by a groggy voice:

VOICE

. . . Hello.

BARTON

Garland, it's me.

GARLAND

Barton? What time is it? Are you all right?

BARTON

Yeah, I'm fine, Garland — I have to talk to you. I'm calling long distance.

GARLAND

Okay.

Muffled, we hear Garland speaking to someone else.

. . . It's Barton. Calling long distance.

Back into the receiver:

. . . What is it Barton? Are you okay?

BARTON

I'm fine, Garland, but I have to talk to you.

GARLAND

Go ahead, son.

BARTON

It's about what I'm writing, Garland. It's really . . . I think it's really big.

GARLAND

What do you mean, Barton?

BARTON

Not big in the sense of large — although it's that too. I mean important. This may be the most *important* work I've done.

GARLAND

Well, I'm . . . glad to hear that —

                         BARTON
Very important, Garland. I just thought you should know
that. Whatever happens.

                         GARLAND
. . . That's fine.

                         BARTON
Have you read the Bible, Garland?

                         GARLAND
. . . Barton, is everything okay?

                         BARTON
Yes . . . Isn't it?

                         GARLAND
Well, I'm just asking. You sound a little –

Guardedly:

                         BARTON
Sound a little what?

                         GARLAND
Well, you just . . . sound a little –

Bitterly:

                         BARTON
Thanks, Garland. Thanks for all the encouragement.

He slams down the phone.

OVER HIS SHOULDER

*A one-quarter shot on Barton from behind as he picks up the
cotton wad and sticks it back in his right ear.*

He resumes typing, furiously.

After a beat he mutters, still typing:

                         BARTON
. . . Nitwit.

THE BATHING BEAUTY

Later. We hear typing and the roar of the surf.

CLOSE ON TYPEWRITER

*We are extremely close on the key-strike area. As we cut in
Barton is typing:*

    p-o-s-t-c-a-r-d-.

*The carriage returns a couple of times and T-H-E − E-N-D is
typed in.*

The paper is ripped out of the carriage.

CLOSE ON A STACK OF PAGES

*Lying face down on the desk; the last page is added, face down, to
the pile.*

*The pile is picked up, its edges are straightened with a couple of
thumps against the desktop, and then the pile is replaced on the
desk, face up.*

The title page reads:

        THE BURLYMAN
    A Motion Picture Scenario
          By
      Barton Fink

*Barton's right hand enters frame to deposit a small cotton wad on
top of the script.*

*Barton's left hand enters to deposit another small cotton wad on
top of the script.*

We hear Barton walk away. We hear bath water run.

THE BATHING BEAUTY

Still looking out to sea.

USO HALL

We are booming down to the dance floor as a raucous swing band plays an up-tempo number.

BARTON

Dancing animatedly, almost manically, his fingers jabbing the air. The hall is crowded, but Barton is one of the few men not in uniform.

USO GIRL

Giggling, dancing opposite Barton.

GIRL

You're cute!

BARTON

Caught up in his dancing, oblivious to the girl.

A white-uniformed arm reaches in to tap Barton on the shoulder.

SAILOR

'Scuse me, buddy, mind if I cut in?

Barton glares at him.

BARTON

This is *my* dance, sailor!

SAILOR

C'mon buddy, I'm shipping out tomorrow.

For some reason Barton is angry.

BARTON

I'm a writer! Celebrating the completion of something *good*! Do you understand that, sailor? I'm a *writer*!

His bellowing has drawn onlookers' attention.

VOICES
Step aside, four-eyes! Let someone else spin the dame!
Give the navy a dance! Hey, Four-F, take a hike!

Barton turns furiously upon the crowd.

BARTON
I'm a writer, you monsters! I *create*!

He points at his head.

. . . This is *my* uniform!

He taps at his skull:

. . . *This* is how I serve the common man! *This* is where
I—

WHAPP! *An infantryman tags Barton's chin on the button.*
Bodies surge. The crowd gasps. The band blares nightmarishly on.

HOTEL HALLWAY

Quiet at the cut.

*After a beat there is a faint ding at the end of the hall and, as
the elevator door opens, we faintly hear:*

PETE
This stop: six.

Barton, disheveled, emerges and stumbles wearily down the hall.
*He stops in front of his door, takes his key out, and enters the
room.*

BARTON'S POV

*Mastrionotti is sitting on the edge of the bed reading Barton's
manuscript.*

Deutsch stands in front of the desk staring at the bathing beauty.

MASTRIONOTTI
(*from the page*)
Mother: What is to become of him. Father: We'll be

hearing from that crazy wrestler. And I don't mean a postcard. Fade out. The end.

He looks up at Barton.

. . . I thought you said you were a writer.

DEUTSCH
I dunno, Duke. I kinda liked it.

BARTON
Keep your filthy eyes off that.

Deutsch turns toward Barton and throws a folded newspaper at him.

DEUTSCH
You made the morning papers, Fink.

Barton opens the paper. A headline reads: Writer Found Headless in Chavez Ravine. The story has two pictures—a studio publicity portrait of Mayhew, and a photograph of the crime scene: Two plainclothes detectives stare down into a gulley as a uniformed cop restrains a pair of leashed dogs.

MASTRIONOTTI
Second one of your friends to wind up dead.

DEUTSCH
You didn't tell us you knew the dame.

With a jerk of his thumb, Mastrionotti indicates the bloodstained bed.

MASTRIONOTTI
Sixth floor too high for you, Fink?

DEUTSCH
Give you nose bleeds?

Barton crosses the room and sits at the foot of the bed, staring at the newspaper.

Just tell me one thing, Fink: Where'd you put their heads?

Distractedly:

BARTON

Charlie . . . Charlie's back . . .

MASTRIONOTTI

No kidding, bright boy—we smelt Mundt all over this.
Was he the idea man?

DEUTSCH

Tell us where the heads are, maybe they'll go easy on you.

MASTRIONOTTI

Only fry you once.

Barton rubs his temples.

BARTON

Could you two come back later? It's just . . . too
hot . . . My head is killing me.

DEUTSCH

All right, forget the heads. Where's Mundt, Fink?

MASTRIONOTTI

He teach you how to do it?

DEUTSCH

You two have some sick sex thing?

BARTON

Sex?! He's a *man*! We *wrestled*!

MASTRIONOTTI

You're a sick fuck, Fink.

DEUTSCH

All right, moron, you're under arrest.

Barton seems oblivious to the two men.

BARTON

Charlie's back. It's hot . . . He's back.

Down the hall we hear the ding of the arriving elevator.

Mastrionotti cocks his head with a quizzical look.

115

He rises and walks slowly out into the hall. Deutsch watches him go.

HIS POV

Mastrionotti in the hallway in full shot, framed by the door, still looking puzzled.

MASTRIONOTTI

. . . Fred . . .

Deutsch stands and pushes his suit coat back past the gun on his hip, revealing a pair of handcuffs on his belt. He unhitches the cuffs and slips one around Barton's right wrist and the other around a loop in the wrought iron footboard of the bed.

DEUTSCH

Sit tight, Fink.

THE HALLWAY

As Deutsch joins Mastrionotti.

DEUTSCH

Why's it so goddamn hot out here?

MASTRIONOTTI

. . . Fred . . .

Deutsch looks where Mastrionotti is looking.

THE WALL

Tacky yellow fluid streams down. The walls are pouring sweat. The hallway is quiet.

MASTRIONOTTI AND DEUTSCH

They look at each other. They look down the hall.

THEIR POV

The elevator stands open at the far end of the empty hall.

For a long beat, nothing.

Finally Pete, the elevator man, emerges.

At this distance he is a small figure, stumbling this way and that, his hands pressed against the sides of his head.

He turns to face Mastrionotti and Deutsch and takes a few hesitant steps forward, still clutching his head.

MASTRIONOTTI AND DEUTSCH

Watching.

PETE

He takes one last step, then collapses.

As he pitches forward his hands fall away from his head. His head separates from his neck, hits the floor, and rolls away from his body with a dull irregular trundle sound.

MASTRIONOTTI AND DEUTSCH

Wide-eyed, they look at each other, then back down the hall.

All is quiet.

THE HALLWAY

Smoke is beginning to drift into the far end of the hall.

We hear a muted rumble.

MASTRIONOTTI AND DEUTSCH

Mastrionotti tugs at his tie. He slowly unholsters his gun. Deutsch slowly, hypnotically, follows suit.

                    DEUTSCH
    . . . Show yourself, Mundt!
More quiet.

THE HALLWAY
More smoke.

LOW STEEP ANGLE ON ELEVATOR DOOR
The crack where the floor of the elevator meets that of the hall.
It flickers with red light from below. Bottom-lit smoke sifts up.

CLOSE ON MASTRIONOTTI
Standing in the foreground, gun at the ready. Sweat pours down
his face.
Behind him, Deutsch stands nervously in the light-spill from
Barton's doorway.
The rumble and crackle of fire grows louder.

THE HALLWAY
More smoke.

PATCH OF WALL
Sweating.
A swath of wallpaper sags away from the top of the wall,
exposing glistening lath underneath.
With a light airy pop, the lathwork catches fire.

MASTRIONOTTI AND DEUTSCH
Sweating.

. . . Mundt!

THEIR POV

The hallway. Its end—facing—wall slowly spreads flame from where the wallpaper droops.

LOW STEEP ANGLE ON ELEVATOR DOOR

More red bottom-lit smoke seeps up from the crack between elevator and hallway floors.

With a groan of tension-relieved cables and a swaying of the elevator floor, a pair of feet crosses the threshold into the hallway.

JUMPING BACK

Wide on the hallway. Charlie Meadows has emerged from the elevator and is hellishly backlit by the flame.

His suit coat hangs open. His hat is pushed back on his head. From his right hand his briefcase dangles.

He stands motionless, facing us. There is something monumental in his posture, shoulders thrown back.

MASTRIONOTTI

Tensed. Behind him, Deutsch gulps.

MASTRIONOTTI
There's a boy, Mundt. Put the policy case down and your mitts in the air.

CHARLIE

He leans slowly down to put the briefcase on the floor.

CLOSE ON MASTRIONOTTI

Relaxing. He murmurs:

MASTRIONOTTI

He's complying.

BACK TO CHARLIE

He straightens up from the briefcase, a sawed-off shotgun in his hands.

BOOM! *The shotgun spits fire.*

Mastrionotti's face is peppered by buckshot and he is blown back down the hallway into Deutsch.

Bellowing fills the hallway over the roar of the fire:

CHARLIE
LOOK UPON ME! LOOK UPON ME! I'LL SHOW
YOU THE LIFE OF THE MIND!!

THE HALLWAY

The fire starts racing down the walls on either side.

CLOSE STEEP ANGLE ON PATCH OF WALL

Fire races along the wall-sweat goopus.

TRACK IN ON DEUTSCH

His eyes widen at Charlie and the approaching fire; his gun dangles forgotten from his right hand.

HIS POV

Charlie is charging down the hallway, holding his shotgun loosely in front of his chest, in double-time position. The fire races along with him.

He is bellowing:

CHARLIE

LOOK UPON ME! I'LL SHOW YOU THE LIFE OF
THE MIND! I'LL SHOW YOU THE LIFE OF THE
MIND!

DEUTSCH

Terrified, he turns and runs.

REVERSE PULLING DEUTSCH

As he runs down the flaming hallway, pursued by flames, smoke, and Karl Mundt – who, also on the run, levels his shotgun.

BOOM!

PUSHING DEUTSCH

His legs and feet sprout blood, paddle futilely at the air, then come down in a twisting wobble, like a car on blown tires, and pitch him helplessly to the floor.

PULLING CHARLIE

He slows to a trot and cracks open the shotgun.

PUSHING DEUTSCH

Weeping and dragging himself forward on his elbows.

PULLING CHARLIE

He slows to a walk.

BARTON'S ROOM

Barton strains at his handcuffs.

HIS POV

Through the open doorway we see Charlie pass, pushing two shells into his shotgun.

PULLING DEUTSCH

Charlie looms behind him and — THWACK — *snaps the shotgun closed.*

Deutsch rolls over to rest on his elbows, facing Charlie.

Charlie primes the shotgun — CLACK.

He presses both barrels against the bridge of Deutsch's nose.

                         CHARLIE
Heil Hitler.

DEUTSCH

Screams.

CHARLIE

Tightens a finger over both triggers. He squeezes.

BLAM.

TRACK IN ON BARTON

He flinches.

The gunshot echoes away.

Barton strains at the handcuffs.

We hear Charlie's footsteps approach — *slowly, heavily.*

THE DOORWAY

Charlie, walking down the hall, glances in and seems mildly surprised to see Barton. The set of his jaw relaxes. His expression softens. He pushes his hat farther back on his head.

CHARLIE

Barton!

He shakes his head and whistles.

. . . Brother, is it hot.

He walks into the room.

BARTON'S ROOM

As Charlie wearily enters.

CHARLIE

How you been, buddy?

He props the shotgun in a corner and sits facing Barton, who stares at him.

. . . Don't look at me like that, neighbor. It's just me—Charlie.

BARTON

I hear it's Mundt. Madman Mundt.

Charlie reaches a flask from his pocket.

CHARLIE

Jesus, people can be cruel . . .

He takes a long draught from the flask, then gives it a haunted stare.

. . . If it's not my build, it's my personality.

Charlie is perspiring heavily. The fire rumbles in the hallway.

. . . They say I'm a madman, Barton, but I'm not mad at anyone. Honest I'm not. Most guys I just feel sorry for. Yeah. It tears me up inside, to think about what they're going through. How trapped they are. I understand it. I feel for 'em. So I try to help them out . . .

He reaches up to loosen his tie and pop his collar button.

. . . Jesus. Yeah. I know what it feels like, when things get all balled up at the head office. It puts you through

123

hell, Barton. So I help people out. I just wish someone would do as much for me . . .

He stares miserably down at his feet.

. . . Jesus, it's hot. Sometimes it gets so hot, I wanna crawl right out of my skin.

Self-pity:

BARTON

But Charlie – why me? Why –

CHARLIE

Because you DON'T LISTEN!

A tacky yellow fluid is dripping from Charlie's left ear and running down his cheek.

. . . Jesus, I'm dripping again.

He pulls some cotton from his pocket and plugs his ear.

. . . C'mon Barton, you think you know about pain? You think I made your life hell? Take a look around this dump. You're just a tourist with a typewriter, Barton. I live here. Don't you understand that . . .

His voice is becoming choked:

And you come into *my* home . . . And you complain that *I'm* making too . . . much . . . noise.

He looks up at Barton.

There is a long silence.

Finally:

BARTON

. . . I'm sorry.

Wearily:

CHARLIE

Don't be.

He rises to his feet and kneels in front of Barton at the foot of the bed.

The two men regard each other.

Charlie grabs two bars of the footboard frame, still staring at Barton. His muscles tighten, though nothing moves. His neck fans with effort. All of his muscles tense. His face is a reddening grimace.

With a shriek of protest, the metal gives. The bar to which Barton is handcuffed has come loose at the top and Barton slides the cuff off it, free.

Charlie gets to his feet.

CHARLIE

I'm getting off this merry-go-round.

He takes his shotgun and walks to the door.

. . . I'll be next door if you need me.

A thought stops him at the door and he turns to face Barton. Behind him the hallway blazes.

. . . Oh, I dropped in on your folks. And Uncle Dave?

He smiles. Barton looks at him dumbly.

. . . Good people. By the way, that package I gave you? I lied. It isn't mine.

He leaves.

Barton rises, picks up Charlie's parcel, and his script.

THE HALLWAY

As Barton emerges. Flames lick the walls, causing the wallpaper to run with the tacky glue sap. Smoke fills the hallway. Barton looks down the hall.

HIS POV

Charlie stands in front of the door to his room, his briefcase dangling from one hand, his other hand fumbling in his pocket for his key.

With his hat pushed back on his head and his shoulders slumped with fatigue, he could be any drummer returning to any hotel after a long hard day on the road.

125

He opens his door and goes into his room.

BACK TO BARTON

He turns to walk up the hallway, his script in one hand, the parcel in the other.

A horrible moaning sound—almost human—can be heard under the roar of the fire.

BLACKNESS

STUDIO HALLWAY

We are tracking laterally across the lobby of an executive building. From offscreen we hear:

BARTON

Fink! Morris or Lillian Fink! Eighty-five Fulton Street!

Filtered through the phone:

OPERATOR

I understand that, sir, but—

BARTON

Or Uncle Dave!

Our track has brought Barton into frame in the foreground, unshaven, unkempt, bellowing into the telephone. In a hallway in the background, a secretary gestures for Barton to hurry it up.

OPERATOR

I understand that, sir, but there's still no answer. Shall I check for trouble on the line?

Barton slams down the phone.

LIPNIK'S OFFICE

Barton enters, still clinging to Charlie's parcel.

Lou Breeze stands in one corner censoriously watching Barton. Lipnik is at the far end of the room, gazing out the window.

LIPNIK

Fink.

BARTON

Mr. Lipnik.

LIPNIK

Colonel Lipnik, if you don't mind.

He turns to face Barton and we see that he is wearing a smartly pressed uniform with a lot of fruit salad on the chest.

. . . Siddown.

Barton takes a seat facing Lipnik's desk.

. . . I was commissioned yesterday in the Army Reserve. Henry Morgenthau arranged it. He's a dear friend.

                                BARTON
Congratulations.

                                LIPNIK
Actually it hasn't officially gone through yet. Had
wardrobe whip this up. You gotta pull teeth to get
anything done in this town. I can understand a little red
tape in peacetime, but now it's all-out warfare against the
Japs. Little yellow bastards. They'd love to see me sit this
one out.

                                BARTON
Yes sir, they—

                                LIPNIK
Anyway. I had Lou read your script for me.

*He taps distastefully at the script on his desk, which has a
slightly charred title page.*

    . . . I gotta tell you, Fink. It won't wash.

                                BARTON
With all due respect, sir, I think it's the best work I've
done.

                                LIPNIK
Don't gas me, Fink. If your opinion mattered, then I guess
I'd resign and let *you* run the studio. It doesn't, and you
won't, and the lunatics are not going to run *this* particular
asylum. So let's put a stop to *that* rumor right now.

Listlessly:

                                BARTON
Yes sir.

                                LIPNIK
I had to call Beery this morning, let him know we were
pushing the picture back. After all I'd told him about
quality, about that Barton Fink feeling. How disappointed
we were. Wally was heartbroken. The man was devastated.
He was—well, *I* didn't actually call him, Lou did. But
that's a fair description, isn't it Lou?

Yes, Colonel.

LIPNIK

Hell, I could take you through it step by step, explain
why your story stinks, but I won't insult your intelligence.
Well all right, first of all: This is a wrestling picture; the
audience wants to see action, drama, wrestling and plenty
of it. They don't wanna see a guy wrestling with his
soul – well all right, a little bit, for the critics – but you
make it the carrot that wags the dog. Too much of it and
they head for the exits and I don't blame 'em. There's
plenty of poetry right inside that ring, Fink. Look at *Hell
Ten Feet Square.*

LOU

Blood, Sweat and Canvas.

LIPNIK

Look at *Blood, Sweat and Canvas.* These are big movies,
Fink. About big men, in tights – both physically and
mentally. But especially physically. We don't put Wallace
Beery in some fruity movie about suffering – I thought we
were together on that.

BARTON

I'm sorry if I let you down.

LIPNIK

You didn't let *me* down. Or even Lou. We don't live or
die by what you scribble, Fink. You let Ben Geisler down.
He liked you. Trusted you. And that's why he's gone.
Fired. That guy had a heart as big as the outdoors, and
you fucked him. He tried to convince me to fire you too,
but that would be too easy. No, you're under contract and
you're gonna stay that way. Anything you write will be the
property of Capitol Pictures. And Capitol Pictures will not
produce anything you write. Not until you grow up a
little. You ain't no writer, Fink – you're a goddamn
write-off.

BARTON

I tried to show you something beautiful. Something about all of *us* —

This sets Lipnik off:

LIPNIK

You arrogant sonofabitch! You think you're the only writer who can give me that Barton Fink feeling?! I got twenty writers under contract that I can ask for a Fink-type thing from. You swell-headed hypocrite! You just don't get it, do you? You still think the whole world revolves around whatever rattles inside that little kike head of yours. Get him out of my sight, Lou. Make sure he stays in town, though; he's still under contract. I want you in town, Fink, and out of my sight. Now get lost. There's a war on.

THE SURF

Crashing against the Pacific shore.

THE BEACH

At midday, almost deserted. In the distance we see Barton walking. The paper-wrapped parcel swings from the twine in his left hand.

BARTON

He walks a few more paces and sits down on the sand, looking out to sea. His gaze shifts to one side.

HIS POV

Down the beach, a bathing beauty walks along the edge of the water. She looks much like the picture on the wall in Barton's hotel room.

BARTON

He stares, transfixed, at the woman.

THE WOMAN

Very beautiful, backlit by the sun, approaching.

BARTON

Following her with his eyes.

THE WOMAN

Her eyes meet Barton's. She says something, but her voice is lost in the crash of the surf.

Barton cups a hand to his ear.

> BEAUTY
>
> I said it's a beautiful day . . .

> BARTON
>
> Yes . . . It is . . .

> BEAUTY
>
> What's in the box?

Barton shrugs and shakes his head.

> BARTON
>
> I don't know.

> BEAUTY
>
> Isn't it yours?

> BARTON
>
> I . . . I don't know . . .

She nods and sits down on the sand several paces away from him, facing the water but looking back over her shoulder at Barton.

> . . . You're very beautiful. Are you in pictures?

She laughs.

Don't be silly.

She turns away to look out at the sea.

WIDER

Facing the ocean. Barton sits in the middle foreground, back to us, the box in the sand next to him.

The bathing beauty sits, back to us, in the middle background.

The surf pounds.

The sun sparkles off the water.

Miller's Crossing

Miller's Crossing was first shown at the New York Film Festival on September 21, 1990.

The cast included:

TOM REAGAN	Gabriel Byrne
VERNA	Marcia Gay Harden
BERNIE BERNBAUM	John Turturro
JOHNNY CASPAR	Jon Polito
EDDIE DANE	J. E. Freeman
LEO	Albert Finney
FRANKIE	Mike Starr
TIC-TAC	Al Mancini
MAYOR DALE LEVANDER	Richard Woods
O'DOOLE	Thomas Toner
MINK	Steve Buscemi
CLARENCE "DROP" JOHNSON	Mario Todisco
TAD	Olek Krupa
ADOLPH	Michael Jeter
TERRY	Lanny Flaherty
MRS. CASPAR	Jeanette Kontomitras
JOHNNY CASPAR, JR.	Louis Charles Mounicou III
COP – BRIAN	John McConnell
COP – DELAHANTY	Danny Aiello III
SCREAMING LADY	Helen Jolly
LANDLADY	Hilda McLean
GUNMEN IN LEO'S HOUSE	Monte Starr
	Don Picard
RUG DANIELS	Salvatore H. Tornabene
STREET URCHIN	Kevin Dearie
CASPAR'S DRIVER	Michael Badalucco
CASPAR'S BUTLER	Charles Ferrara
CASPAR'S COUSINS	Esteban Fernandez
	George Fernandez
HITMAN AT VERNA'S	Charles Gunning
HITMAN NO. 2	Dave Drinkx
LAZARRE'S MESSENGER	David Darlow

LAZARRE'S TOUGHS	Robert LaBrosse
	Carl Rooney
MAN WITH PIPE BOMB	Jack David Harris
SON OF ERIN	Jery Hewitt
SNICKERING GUNMAN	Sam Raimi
COP WITH BULLHORN	John Schnauder, Jr.
RABBI	Zolly Levin
BOXERS	Joey Ancona
	Bill Raye

And Featuring the	
Remarkable Voice of	William Preston Robertson
Directed by	Joel Coen
Produced by	Ethan Coen
Written by	Joel Coen and Ethan Coen
Co-Producer	Mark Silverman
Associate Producer	Graham Place
Executive Producer	Ben Barenholtz
Director of Photography	Barry Sonnenfeld
Production Designer	Dennis Gassner
Costume Designer	Richard Hornung
Music Composed by	Carter Burnwell
Edited by	Michael Miller
Supervising Sound Editor	Skip Lievsay
Dialogue Supervisor	Philip Stockton
Casting by	Donna Isaacson, C.S.A. &
	John Lyons, C.S.A.

Released by Twentieth Century Fox Film Corporation.

A WHISKEY TUMBLER

It sits on an oak bar under a glowing green banker's lamp. Two ice cubes are dropped in. From elsewhere in the room:

> MAN (*off*)
> I'm talkin' about friendship. I'm talkin' about character. I'm talkin' about—hell, Leo, I ain't embarrassed to use the word—I'm talkin' about ethics.

Whiskey is poured into the tumbler, filling it almost to the rim, as the offscreen voice continues.

> . . . You know I'm a sporting man. I like to make the occasional bet. But I ain't *that* sporting.

THE SPEAKER

A balding middle-aged man with a round, open face. He sits, overcoated, in a leather chair in the dark room, softly illuminated by an offscreen desk lamp. He is JOHNNY CASPAR.

Behind him stands another man, harder looking, wearing an overcoat and hat and holding another hat—presumably Caspar's. This is EDDIE DANE.

> CASPAR
> When I fix a fight, say—if I pay a three-to-one favorite to throw a goddamn fight—I figure I got a right to expect that fight to go off at three-to-one. But every time I lay a bet with this sonofabitch Bernie Bernbaum, before I know it the odds is even up—or worse, I'm betting the short money . . .

Behind Caspar we hear the clink of ice in the tumbler and a figure approaches from the bar glowing in the background.

> . . . The sheeny knows I like sure things. He's selling the information I fixed the fight. Out-of-town money comes pourin' in. The odds go straight to hell. I don't know who

he's sellin' it to, maybe the Los Angeles combine, I don't know. The point is, Bernie ain't satisfied with the honest dollar he can make off the vig. He ain't satisfied with the business I do on his book. He's sellin' tips on how I bet, and that means part of the payoff that should be ridin' on my hip is ridin' on someone else's. So back we go to these questions – friendship, character, ethics.

The man with the whiskey glass has just passed the camera and we cut to the:

REVERSE

Another well-dressed middle-aged man sits behind a large polished oak desk, listening. This is LEO. *He is short but powerfully built, with the face of a man who has seen things.*

The man with the whiskey enters frame and passes Leo to lean against the wall behind him.

CASPAR
So it's clear what I'm saying?

LEO
. . . As mud.

Caspar purses his lips, but continues.

CASPAR
It's a wrong situation. It's gettin' so a businessman can't expect no return from a fixed fight. Now, if you can't trust a fix, what *can* you trust? For a good return you gotta go bettin' on chance, and then you're back with anarchy. Right back inna jungle. On account of the breakdown of ethics. That's why ethics is important. It's the grease makes us get along, what separates us from the animals, beasts a burden, beasts a prey. Ethics. Whereas Bernie Bernbaum is a horse of a different color ethics-wise. As in, he ain't got any.

Leo leans back in his chair.

The man behind Leo raises the whiskey glass to his lips.

140

He is younger and trimmer than Leo, perhaps in his thirties, dark-complected, with a pencil mustache and a gaunt intensity that is not entirely healthy-looking. This is TOM REAGAN.

As he drinks, he studies Caspar and Eddie Dane.

                    LEO
You sure it's Bernie, selling you out?

For the first time the man behind Caspar speaks:

                    DANE
It ain't elves.

                    LEO
Nobody else knows about the fix?

                    CASPAR
No one that ain't got ethics.

                    LEO
What about the fighters you pay to tank out?

                    DANE
We only pick fighters we can put the fear of God in.

                    LEO
Any other bookies know? You play anyone else's book?

                    CASPAR
I lay an occasional bet with Mink Larouie.

                    DANE
But it ain't Mink, I'll vouch for that.

                    LEO
How do you know?

Caspar shakes his head.

                    CASPAR
It ain't Mink. Mink is Eddie Dane's boy.

                    LEO
Mm. And of course, the Dane always knows about the fix.

                    DANE
What the hell is that supposed to mean?

LEO

Let it drift. All it means is a lot of people know.

CASPAR

I guess you ain't been listening. Sure, other people know.
That's why we gotta go to this question of character,
determine just who exactly is chiseling in on my fix. And
that's how we know it's Bernie Bernbaum. The Shmatte
Kid. 'Cause ethically, he's kinda shaky.

LEO

You know Bernie's chiseling you because he's a chiseler.
And you know he's a chiseler because he's chiseling you.

CASPAR
(airily)

Sometimes you just know.

LEO

. . . So you wanna kill him.

DANE

For starters.

Leo nods, thinking. He swivels to look interrogatively at Tom.

*Tom gives an almost imperceptible shrug. The ice cubes in his
glass clink.*

Leo turns back to Caspar, pauses.

LEO

. . . Sorry, Caspar. Bernie pays me for protection.

Tom, peering over his drink, does not entirely conceal his surprise.

*Caspar stares at Leo, his mouth open. It is not the answer he
expected either.*

CASPAR

. . . Listen, Leo, I ain't askin' for permission. I'm tellin'
you as a courtesy. I need to do this thing, so it's gonna get
done.

LEO

Then I'm telling you as a courtesy you'll have trouble.
You came here to see if I'd kick if you killed Bernie; well,
there's your answer.

Caspar's voice is harder:

CASPAR

Listen, Leo, I pay off to you every month like a
greengrocer – a lot more than the Shmatte – and I'm sick a
gettin' the high hat –

LEO

You pay off for protection, just like everyone else. Far as I
know – and what I don't know in this town ain't worth

knowing – the cops haven't closed any of your dives and the D.A. hasn't touched any of your rackets. You haven't bought any license to kill bookies and today I ain't selling any. Now take your flunky and dangle.

Caspar rises slowly to his feet.

CASPAR

Ya know I'm tryin' . . . I'm tryin' not to raise my voice in anger. But you make me lay off the Shmatte and you're givin' me the needle. I told you the sheeny was robbin' me blind, I told you I wanna put him in the ground, and I'm tellin' you now I'm sick a the high hat.

He swipes his hat from the Dane.

. . . You think I'm some guinea fresh off the boat and you think you can kick me. But I'm too big for that now.

He puts his hands on the desk and leans in toward Leo. The cords on his neck stand out.

I'm sick a takin' the strap from you, Leo. I'm sick a marchin' down to this goddamn office to kiss your Irish ass and I'M SICK A THE HIGH HAT!

Caspar stops, out of breath. He is red-faced and panting. The Dane has put a gently restraining hand on his shoulder.

Leo and Tom stare impassively at Caspar.

After a beat Caspar closes his mouth. His eyes lose some of their glaze. He looks at Eddie Dane's hand, turns and strides toward the door.

Youse fancy-pants, all of yas.

He opens the door but Leo's voice stops him.

LEO
(*softly*)

Johnny. You're exactly as big as I let you be and no bigger and don't forget it. Ever.

Caspar looks at Leo from the open doorway. After a beat he chuckles.

CASPAR

Ats right, Leo, you're the big shot around here.

He glances over at Tom, then back at Leo:

. . . And I'm just some shnook likes to get slapped around.

He leaves, Eddie Dane following.

After a beat Tom crosses in front of the desk and sits in Caspar's chair, facing Leo. Leo chuckles and leans back.

LEO

Twist a pig's ear. Watch him squeal.

Tom swallows the last of his drink and stares ruminatively down at the glass.

TOM

. . . Bad play, Leo.

Leo, unfazed, grins at Tom.

LEO

Got up on the wrong side, huh?

TOM

Same side as always.

LEO

That's what I mean. Still owe money to – who's your bookie? Lazarre?

TOM

Mm.

LEO

I could put it right for you.

TOM

Thanks, Leo, I don't need it.

LEO

In a pig's eye. You haven't played a winner in six weeks.
People'll speak ill of me if I let him break your legs.

Tom grins back, for the first time.

TOM

People'll say I had it coming.

LEO

And they'll be right, but that ain't the point. Call me a
big-hearted slob but I'm gonna square it for you.

He picks up a phone on his desk and starts to dial.

. . . Yeah, I think I'll do that, this very same night.
Looking at you moping around takes away all my—what
do you call it? Joy de veever?

Tom walks over to the desk.

TOM

Joie de vivre.

He takes the receiver from Leo and prongs it.

LEO

Well look, if you're gonna laugh at me, the hell with you.

Tom walks to the door, putting on his hat.

TOM

And with you. I'll square myself with Lazarre if you don't
mind. That's why God invented cards.

He pauses in the doorway.

. . . There is something you can do for me.

LEO

Name it.

TOM

Think about what protecting Bernie gets us. Think about
what offending Caspar loses us.

Leo chuckles.

146

LEO

Come on, Tommy, you know I don't like to think.

Tom has stepped into the hallway and, just as he closes the door:

TOM

Yeah. Well, think about whether you should start.

The door clicks shut.

CUT TO BLACK

FADE IN:
WOODS

Although it is day, the tree cover gives an effect of cathedral-like darkness. Sun filters down through the leaves in gently shifting patterns.

We hear only the sound of the wind and the creaking and groaning of tree limbs in the breeze.

Head titles are supered over the dissolving series of woods scenes.

In the last scene the angle is low — almost ground-level. The sun dapples the floor of the forest, which is carpeted with pine needles.

With a whoosh of rustling leaves the wind gusts a fedora into frame. For a moment it lies still in the foreground, sunlight rippling over it, making it seem almost alive. Then the wind picks up again and the hat tumbles away from us, in slow motion, end over end into the background until . . . it disappears.

Under a fade out, we hear a distant knocking.

CLOSE SHOT   TOM

Unshaven, eyes closed, motionless.

The knocking continues, faintly, offscreen. As we hear a door opening we pull back to a looser shot, revealing that Tom is slumped back on a sagging green sofa.

147

A fat hand enters to shake Tom's shoulder.

> VOICE

Wake up, Tommy.

Without opening his eyes:

> TOM

I am awake.

> VOICE

Your eyes were shut.

> TOM

Who're you gonna believe?

Tom sits up, though it seems an effort. He looks sick. A small mirror behind the couch shows that we are in the back room of a gambling establishment. The leavings of a card game litter a table in the middle background.

. . . How'd I do?

> VOICE

What do you think. You're a millionaire. You gonna remember your friends?

Tom reaches up to feel his head, and looks stupidly about.

> TOM

. . . Where's my hat?

> VOICE

You bet it, mug. Good thing the game broke up before you bet your trousers.

After a beat of staring at nothing in particular, Tom abruptly lurches to his feet and staggers out of frame.

The other man sits heavily onto the couch that Tom has just left. He is FAT TONY, *a big man wearing an apron.*

He watches as we hear Tom, offscreen, staggering across the room, bumping into something which scrapes and clatters to the floor, opening a door, staggering across tile, and vomiting.

Fat Tony watches with mild interest.
Finally:

TOM (*off*)
. . . Who left with my hat?

TONY
Verna. Verna and Mink.

TOM (*off*)
. . . Who?

Louder:

TONY
Mink and Verna.

We hear a tap running.

TOM (*off*)
. . . Thunderclap running tonight?

TONY
Yeah.

TOM (*off*)
What's she leave at?

TONY
Three-to-one, more'n likely. Lay off, Tom. You shouldn't
go deeper in the hole.

TOM (*off*)
Tell Lazarre I want five hundred on the nose.

Fat Tony shrugs.

TONY
You would have it.

TOM (*off*)
. . . Somebody hit me?

TONY
Yeah. Mink hit you.

TOM (*off*)
. . . Whyzat?

149

Fat Tony inspects a hangnail.

> TONY
>
> You asked him to.

HALLWAY

A loose shot over Tom's shoulder. He knocks on an apartment door.

The door swings open and VERNA, *a woman in her late twenties or early thirties, looks coldly out.*

> TOM
>
> I want my hat.

> VERNA
>
> . . . Is that all you came for?

> TOM
>
> Yeah. I want my hat.

> VERNA
>
> I won it. It's mine.

> TOM
>
> What're *you* gonna do with it?

> VERNA
>
> Drop dead.

She slams the door.

There is a long, motionless beat. Tom raises his hand and knocks again, missing the door completely on his first try.

After a knock or two the door swings open again.

> TOM
>
> I need a drink.

> VERNA
>
> Why didn't you say so?

She steps away from the door and Tom enters.

150

CLOSE SHOT   A FEDORA

It lies on a marble bureau top in a dark room. A gently rippling cookie plays over it — light from a streetlamp thrown through a curtained window. Reflected in the bureau mirror behind the hat is the soft glow of a burning cigarette.

REVERSE

Tracking in on Tom, sitting in bed, smoking, staring at the bureau. The rippling street light plays over him. We hear a distant knocking.

WIDER

Tom swings his legs around and gets out of bed.

He throws on a dressing gown and leaves the bedroom through its double oak pocket doors, closing the doors behind him.

LIVING ROOM

The knocking is louder here. Silhouetted against the streetlit windows, Tom crosses the room to the front door. Light fans in as he opens it.

Shifting uncomfortably in the hallway is Leo, in an overcoat and fedora.

>   LEO
> 'Lo, Tommy. Sorry about the hour.

>   TOM
> I'll live. What's the rumpus?

>   LEO
> Can I come in?

Tom thinks about this for the slightest beat.

>   TOM
> Sure.

He lets Leo precede him into the living room.

Tom turns on a lamp that sits on a rolling bar.

   . . . Drink?

TOM

LEO

I wouldn't mind . . . I tried calling earlier.

TOM

I got home late.

Tom gives Leo his drink and sits facing him with his own.

LEO

Well . . . Sorry about the hour.

TOM

Uh-huh.

He waits, with no apparent impatience.

The older man is uncomfortable; he is having trouble finding the words. Finally he lifts his glass and swallows the drink in one gulp.

LEO

. . . Not bad.

TOM

Better than the paint we sell at the club.

LEO

That it is . . . That it is . . .

TOM

Thought about cutting Bernie loose?

Leo is shuffling his hat from hand to hand.

LEO

Can't do it, Tommy, can't do it . . . That's sort of why I'm . . . Tommy . . . I don't know where Verna is.

Tom gives him a level stare, then takes a sip of his drink.

TOM

Uh-huh.

LEO

I know what you're thinking: What else is new? But the situation now, I'm worried.

TOM

Verna can take care of herself. Maybe better than you can.

LEO

What does that mean?

Tom stands, takes Leo's glass, and walks back over to the bar.

TOM

Want another?

LEO

No. What does that mean?

Tom turns to look at Leo, pauses, then decides to speak:

TOM

How far has she got her hooks into you?

LEO

That's a hell of a question.

TOM

It's a grift, Leo. If she didn't need you to protect her brother from Johnny Caspar, d'you think she'd still go with you on slow carriage rides through the park? That is the deal, isn't it? You keep Bernie under wraps till Caspar cools down?

LEO

Jesus, but you're a prickly pear. What's wrong with her wanting her brother taken care of?

TOM

Not a thing. I don't blame *her*. She sees the angle – which is you – and she plays it. She's a grifter, just like her brother. They probably had grifter parents and grifter grandparents and someday they'll each spawn little grifter kids –

LEO

Stop it, Tommy. I don't like to hear my friends run down. Even by other friends.

Tom shrugs.

TOM

Friendship's got nothing to do with it.

LEO

The hell you say. You do anything to help your friends.
Just like you do anything to kick your enemies.

TOM

Wrong, Leo. You do things for a reason.

LEO

Okay, Tom, you know the angles – Christ, better than
anybody. But you're wrong about this. You don't know
what's in Verna's heart.

Tom stares down into his drink.

TOM

. . . Leo, throw her down. And her brother too. Dump
her.

Leo looks like he has just been stepped on.

LEO

Jesus, Tom . . . Verna's okay . . .

He nods to himself.

. . . She's a little wild, but she's okay. I like her.

TOM

Yeah, you like her. Like the Kaiser likes cabbage. You're
dizzy for her.

LEO

What of it? Jesus, Tom, ain't you ever been bit by that
bug?

TOM

Leo, if she's such an angel why are you looking for her at
four in the morning?

*Leo digs his hands into his pockets and slouches back, profoundly
embarrassed.*

154

LEO

. . . I put a tail on her this afternoon.

TOM

Hah!

LEO

Yeah, I asked Rug Daniels to follow her around – just, you know, just to keep her out of trouble.

TOM

And to tell you what trouble she was managing to whip up herself.

LEO

It wasn't to spy, Tom; I was worried. After that meeting with Caspar, well – you can't be too careful.

TOM

Uh-huh. And what did Rug tell you that has you scurrying over here?

LEO

That's just it. Nothing. He's disappeared.

Tom laughs humorlessly.

TOM

So you've lost your ladyfriend *and* the tail you put on her.

LEO

I guess it does sound pretty sorry at that . . .

He looks from his empty glass to Tom.

. . . Help me out, Tom. I wouldn't know where to start looking. You know Rug's crowd, you know the people Verna runs with. I'm just worried now, with things the way they are between me and Caspar –

Tom gives a wave of disgust.

TOM

You shouldn't be confronting Johnny Caspar, it's what I've been trying to tell you. You can't trade body blows with him. He's gotten too strong.

155

For the first time Leo displays some testiness:

                                LEO
I reckon I can still trade body blows with any man in this
town . . .

He sighs, looks back down at his drink.

    . . . Except you, Tom.

                                TOM
And Verna.

Leo smiles good-naturedly.

                                LEO
Okay, give me the needle. I *am* a sap, I deserve it . . .

He stands and walks to the door.

Tom doesn't move. His eyes remain fixed on Leo's empty chair.

Leo pauses in the open door.

    . . . Thanks for the drink. Let me know if you hear
anything.

The door closes and he is gone.

*Tom grimaces and stands. Sunlight is just starting to come in
through the windows, defining for the first time all of the large
semicircular room as Tom walks across it to the bedroom. Early-
morning traffic noise is filtering up from the street.*

BEDROOM

Tom opens the double oak doors and enters, leaving them open.

*He crosses to the bed and sits on its edge, hunched forward,
thinking. Behind him, a woman stirs.*

                            WOMAN
                           (*sleepily*)
Who was that?

                                TOM
Leo . . .

                                156

He takes a cigarette from the nightstand and lights it.

. . . He's looking for you.

Verna stiffens.

VERNA

Did you tell him I was here?

TOM

No.

Verna relaxes.

VERNA

Did you put in a good word for my brother?

TOM

No.

VERNA

You said you would.

TOM

. . . I said I'd think about it.

VERNA

What *did* you tell him?

Tom is lost in thought. He exhales smoke.

TOM

. . . Did you see Rug Daniels last night?

VERNA

No. What did you tell Leo?

Tom finally turns to face her. After looking at her for a beat:

TOM

. . . I told him you were a tramp and he should dump you.

A shoe flies past his head and hits the wall behind him.

VERNA

You're a sonofabitch, Tom.

ALLEY – EARLY MORNING

*We are on a close shot of a small dog. Behind him, in the
distance, is the mouth of the alley.*

*The dog is pointing, perfectly still, one front leg crooked and
raised off the ground, his ears straight up, his eyes in a fixed
stare.*

A MAN

*Slouched, half-sitting, against the wall of the alley. He is
motionless. His mouth is agape. His eyes are rolled up in a
lifeless stare.*

*He is wearing an overcoat, but it is unbuttoned and reveals a
blood stain in the middle of his chest. His fedora lies on the
ground near one of his splayed hands.*

There is something subtly odd about his hair.

A LITTLE BOY

Five years old. He stares down at the dead man in front of him.

THE MAN

Staring vacantly.

THE BOY

After a moment, he reaches forward.

THE MAN

*The boy's hand enters frame. The boy pokes once at the man's
shoulder.*

There is no reaction.

The boy touches the top of the man's head.

The man's hair slips forward a couple of inches over his forehead.

THE BOY

Staring.

THE MAN

Also staring, his skewed hairpiece ill becoming his stunned expression.

The boy reaches forward and takes the hairpiece off the man's head. Now a bald man stares off into space, still looking stunned, still quite dead.

WIDE SHOT   THE ALLEY

The dead man and the little boy face each other in profile in the middle foreground. In the background, between them, the little boy's dog faces us, still pointing, still whining.

The little boy is fascinated by the hairpiece he holds. He turns it over and around, and looks from it to the dead man.

Suddenly the boy turns and runs away toward the mouth of the alley, clutching the hairpiece.

As he passes the dog it turns and runs after him, wagging its tail, happy to be leaving.

FADE OUT

FADE IN:
DINER – DUSK

A man sits facing us at the counter in the foreground. His face is hidden by the newspaper he reads.

The page of the newspaper being presented to the camera bears a story headlined: GANGSTER SLAIN. *The subhead: Politician's "Aide" Found Dead in Alley.*

After a beat the diner drops the paper to the counter and we see that it is Tom. He is grimacing at what he was reading. He stands and digs into his pocket.

REVERSE

Looking down at the newspaper on the counter, next to a steaming cup of coffee. Tom's hand enters to put some change on the counter, leaves, and we hear his receding footsteps.

The headlined story on the page Tom was reading is: THUNDERCLAP INJURED IN RACING MISHAP.

TRACKING IN TO CLOSE SHOT   PLAQUE

Set into the brick of a building's exterior, it reads: SHENANDOAH CLUB. *In script underneath: Members Only.*

INT. LEO'S CLUB

Tracking toward the front door as Tom enters. He puts his coat and hat on the check counter.

TOM

Hello, Beryl—

An arm sweeps across frame to slap Tom hard.

CHECK GIRL (*off*)

Ain't you got a conscience?

Tom stares dumbly.

BERYL

She is a small woman in a French maid's uniform and a pillbox hat. She rocks her weight back onto one leg with her hands propped defiantly on her hips.

. . . It's a little voice inside that tells you when you been a heel!

TOM

What'd I do?

BERYL

Stood me up is all! Made me wait an hour and a half is all! Or maybe you don't remember sayin' you'd pick me up after work last night. I seen heels in my time, sure, plenty of 'em! But none so low as couldn't tell me to my face when they was sick of me!

She throws a check number at him.

. . . You know where you can stick it!

TRACKING SHOT

Pulling Tom as he walks across the gambling floor. He is joined by a nervous young man in a tuxedo.

MINK

'Lo Tom. What's the rumpus?

TOM

Mink.

Mink throws a glance back in the direction of the coat check.

MINK

I see you got your hat back.

TOM

Yeah, what of it.

MINK

Not a thing, Tommy. If it ain't my business I got not a thing to say. Listen, Bernie wants to see you. It's important.

TOM

Well I'm right here, and I'm not made of glass.

MINK

Yeah, but he's nervous walkin' around in public. He's a right guy, but he's nervous, Tommy! He's very nervous! Who wouldn't be?!

Tom looks at Mink for the first time.

TOM

Mink—

MINK

The spot he's in, who wouldn't be! He asked me to ask you to ask Leo to take care of him. You know, put in a good word with Leo. Leo listens to you. Not that Leo wouldn't help the Shmatte anyway! A guy like Bernie? A square gee like the Shmatte? A straight shooter like him?

TOM

I don't get it, Mink—

MINK

What's to get?! It's as plain as the nose—

TOM

I thought you were Eddie Dane's sycophant.

MINK

Yeah, Tom, that's right. But a guy can have more than one friend, can't he? Not that I'd want the Dane to know about it, but a square gee like the Shmatte? He's a right guy, Tom! He's a straight shooter! I know he's got a

162

mixed reputation, but for a sheeny he's got a lot a good qualities!

Tom has reached the foot of a large staircase. He turns to look curiously at Mink.

TOM

What's going on between you and Bernie?

MINK

Nothin', Tom! We're just friends – you know, amigos?

He sips on his cigarette and looks nervously around the floor.

TOM

You're a fickle boy, Mink. If the Dane found out you had another "amigo" – well, I don't peg him for the understanding type.

Mink is startled. As Tom walks up the stairs Mink calls after him in a piping voice:

MINK

Find out!? How would he find out?! Damnit, Tom, me and you ain't even been talking! Jesus, Tom, damnit, Jesus!

LEO'S OFFICE

Pulling Tom as he enters.

LEO (*off*)

'Lo, Tom. You know O'Doole . . .

REVERSE

Leo faces us from behind his desk.

Seated in two chairs facing the desk, twisting around to greet Tom, are two men. O'DOOLE *is a large man in a police uniform.* DALE LEVANDER *wears a suit; he is a florid man in his mid-sixties with a shock of white hair.*

LEO

. . . and the mayor.

TOM

I ought to. I voted for him six times last May.

Levander chuckles.

LEVANDER

And that ain't the record, either.

Tom is crossing to the bar.

LEO

Verna turned up. She's downstairs.

Tom, his back to Leo as he pours a drink, stiffens.

TOM

. . . She say where she'd been?

LEO

No, I uh . . . didn't want to press her. Hear about Rug?

Drink in hand, Tom turns and crosses to perch on a corner of Leo's desk.

TOM

Yeah, R.I.P.

LEO

They took his hair, Tommy. Jesus, that's strange. Why would they do that?

TOM

Maybe it was Injuns.

LEO

Eye-ties, more like it. Giovanni Gasparro.

TOM

So you figure it was Caspar bumped Rug?

Leo glances at O'Doole and the mayor with an indulgent smile, then back at Tom.

LEO

. . . Well it's pretty obvious, ain't it?

TOM

Mm . . . So what's the plan?

Jump on the guinea hard. With both feet.

He looks at the mayor, who shifts uncomfortably.

. . . Give him the low-down, Dale.

MAYOR

Yes, well, Leo here has just reminded us that Mr. Caspar operates several clubs in our city wherein the patrons imbibe of rum and play at games of chance.

O'DOOLE
(*morosely*)

And we're supposed to stop the party.

TOM

Uh-huh . . .

Looking at Leo, he jerks his head toward the two men.

. . . They don't seem too happy about it, Leo.

O'DOOLE

Naw, it ain't that, Tom.

MAYOR

Jesus, Tom! We do as we're told!

TOM

Maybe they're right not to like it. Stirring up this hornets' nest won't be good for anyone. And it'll mean killing.

LEO

Well I'm not thrilled about it either, but I can't just lay down to Caspar.

TOM

You could do worse. You might not like it, but giving up Bernie Bernbaum is a pretty small price to pay for peace. Business is business and a war's going to hurt everybody. Bernie plays with fire, he's got to deal with the consequences – even if that means he gets bumped off.

Sweet Jesus, Tom, that ain't even the point anymore.
Caspar pooped Rug. The day I back down from a fight
Caspar is welcome to the rackets, this town, and my place
at the table. I didn't start this thing, but—

Tom's voice is sharp:

TOM

You *did* start it—you and Verna—

The mayor has risen uncomfortably to his feet.

MAYOR

We can dangle, Leo, if you'd prefer.

LEO

Siddown, Dale, we're all friends here.

TOM

—and Caspar hasn't broken the rules, Bernie has—and
you, too, by helping him. And if that isn't enough,
consider that if you make it a war, you've more to lose
than Caspar.

*Leo is getting up from behind the desk and walking over to stare
out the window.*

LEO

Okay, but more to beat him with. Jesus, Tom, the two of
us've faced worse odds.

TOM

But never without reason. It helps to have one.

Leo doesn't reply. Tom is irritated, but shrugs indifference.

. . . Well, it's your call.

He gets to his feet and heads for the door.

. . . My opinion used to count for something around
here, but it's always yours to take or leave.

*Leo has turned from the window and is striding after Tom,
gesturing apologetically.*

                        LEO
Aw, c'mon Tommy. It's not like that . . .

The door clicks shut.

        . . . Goddamnit. Goddamn kid is just like a twist.

FAT TONY

He tends the downstairs bar as Tom stalks over.

                        TOM
Gimme a stiff one.

                        TONY
No small talk, huh? They shoot your nag?

*Tony has finished pouring a shot of whiskey which Tom
immediately knocks back.*

                        TOM
If there's any justice. Verna around?

                        TONY
She stepped into the ladies' room. You got Lazarre's five
hundred?

                        TOM
He'll have to carry me for a few days.

Tom is pouring himself another drink.

                        TONY
He ain't gonna like that. Couldn't you get it from Leo?

Tom is irritated:

                        TOM
It's not Leo's debt. I'll pay my own way.

                        TONY
I admire a man of principle. Does this go on the tab?

Tom is already walking away.

                        167

LADIES' LOUNGE

Tom bangs through the door, still carelessly holding his tumbler of whiskey. A rogue lock of hair hangs down over his forehead.

TOM
Close your eyes, ladies, I'm coming through.

REVERSE

The hubbub of female voices subsides as all turn to look at the male intruder.

The lounge is done in various shades of pink. Some women apply makeup facing large bulb-encircled mirrors in overstuffed seashell-shaped pink chairs. Other women sit, smoking, in the banquettes that line the other wall.

All react to Tom's entrance with surprise and outrage, and they hurry to gather their things and leave. The one exception is Verna, who looks at Tom with unperturbed distaste.

As he crosses to her seashell chair:

TOM
Who's the war paint for?

VERNA
Go home and dry out.

TOM
You don't need it for Leo, believe me. He already thinks you're the original Miss Jesus.

She glances hurriedly around the lounge, but the last of the women are already leaving.

VERNA
. . . What the hell's the matter with you?

TOM
What's the matter with you? Afraid people might get the right idea?

168

VERNA

Leo's got the right idea. I like him, he's honest and he's got a heart.

Tom weaves a couple of steps closer.

TOM

Then it's true what they say. Opposites attract.

VERNA

Do me a favor and mind your own business.

She turns back to the mirror and starts applying lipstick. Tom drops down to face her in the mirror.

TOM

This is my business. Intimidating helpless women is part of what I do.

VERNA

Then find one and intimidate her.

Tom swallows the rest of his drink.

TOM

Leo's upstairs getting ready to shoot himself in the foot on your account.

VERNA

I don't know what you're talking about.

TOM

He's gonna go to the mat for your brother. And it's gonna hurt him.

VERNA

I don't know Leo's business, but he's a big boy.

TOM

He used to be.

Verna pauses with the lipstick.

VERNA

Look. What do you want, Tom? You want me to pretend I don't care what happens to Bernie? Well, I do. He's my brother and I don't want him to get hurt. If Leo wants to

169

help him out I'll step out with him, show him a good time in return. There's no harm in that.

TOM

There's a name for that kind of business arrangement.

VERNA

I'll do what I have to for Bernie and there's no reason for you to try and queer that. Regardless of what you think of me, Bernie's a decent guy.

TOM

A straight shooter, huh? A square gee?

VERNA

Yeah, sneer at him like everyone else. Just because he's different. People think he's a degenerate. People think he's scum. Well, he's not.

TOM

Poor misunderstood Bernie.

Verna swivels to look quizzically at Tom.

VERNA

. . . What is this about? You want me to stop seeing Leo, why don't you just say so?

TOM

I want you to quit spinning Leo in circles and pointing him where to go.

VERNA

I forgot—that's *your* job, isn't it?

TOM

I'll do what *I* have to to protect Leo. I'm asking you to leave him alone. I don't *have* to ask. If I told him about our little dance last night, your pull would dry up pretty fast.

Now Verna is irritated:

VERNA

So would yours. I don't like being threatened.

TOM

And I don't like being played for a sucker. That game might work with Leo, but it won't work with me.

VERNA

You think last night was just more campaigning for my brother?

TOM

I can see the angles . . .

He grabs her and drags her roughly to her feet.

. . . And I know if there was a market for little old ladies, you'd have Grandma Bernbaum first on line.

She struggles to escape.

VERNA

You're a pathetic rumhead.

TOM

And I love you, angel.

Tom takes her hat off, tosses it onto the chair, and kisses her.

Verna breaks away and socks him on the jaw.

Tom staggers back, upsetting a table of toiletries and landing against a banquette.

He throws his whiskey glass at Verna.

She ducks and it smashes into the mirror.

They stand staring at each other for a beat, panting. Tom has a smear of lipstick near one side of his mouth.

Finally:

VERNA

I suppose you think you've raised hell.

She picks up her stole and heads for the door.

Tom, swaying ever so slightly, watches her go.

TOM

. . . Sister, when I've raised hell you'll know it.

TOM'S APARTMENT

A wide shot, facing the semicircular windows, the door of the apartment behind us. A large easy chair in the middle foreground faces away from us; a smaller chair is at the window end of the room, facing us.

At the cut we hear the ringing of the telephone.

Offscreen we hear the unhurried scrape of a key in the lock, then the door opening, then the door closing.

Tom's back enters frame as he strolls into the room and then disappears briefly through an open doorway to the right. We hear an icebox door opening and closing, and then Tom reenters, still not reacting to the insistently ringing phone. He is now holding a balled-up towel.

He walks over to the facing chair at the window end of the room, shrugs off his overcoat, drapes it on the chair, sits, crosses his legs, takes off his hat, tosses it onto the upraised toes of his crossed leg,

172

tilts his head back, and presses the towel against his forehead. Apparently it is an icepack.

We track slowly toward him.

After a beat he takes out a cigarette, lights it, and reaches back for the phone that refuses to stop ringing.

TOM

Yeah . . .

He looks casually forward at a specific point in space. He does not react to whatever he is hearing.

. . . I need a couple of days . . . Because I don't have it now . . .

We are almost in close shot. Tom's gaze remains fixed and emotionless.

. . . Because I say so . . . What *would* be good enough? . . . Well, if it'll make him feel any better, tell Lazarre he can send someone by to break my legs. I won't squawk.

He prongs the earpiece, still looking off. The track has stopped in close shot. He exhales a stream of smoke; then, after a beat:

. . . 'Lo, Bernie.

REVERSE

Slouched, smiling, in a chair facing Tom is BERNIE BERNBAUM. *He is about thirty and wears his overcoat and hat and holds an apple in one hand and a paring knife in the other. The long peel of the apple corkscrews down off the knife.*

BERNIE

'Lo, Tom. What's the rumpus?

TOM

C'mon in, make yourself at home.

173

BERNIE

Yeah, you weren't here so I thought I'd do that. Didn't wanna answer the phone, though. Figured it wasn't for me.

TOM

Uh-huh.

After a silent beat, Bernie chuckles.

BERNIE

. . . I get it, get to the point, huh? Okay. The point is: I'm a good guy.

TOM

I've heard that from a lot of people today.

Bernie slices off an apple section and holds it out to Tom, who shakes his head.

> BERNIE
> Good guy, lot of friends – that's the way it works. Maybe if you appreciated me a little more, you wouldn't be making waves with Leo.

He pops the slice into his mouth.

> It's a bad time to be doing that. I mean, right now we're both in a jam. I hear you're on a bad streak, short of funds, and I've got that crazy dago mad at me. Don't ask me why; I'm just a small-timer trying to get by, like everyone else. I need help from my friends. Like Leo. And you.

> TOM
> Leo gets your sister; what're you selling me?

> BERNIE
> C'mon Tom, it's not like that at all. Wasn't my idea, she'll sleep with anyone, you know that. She's even tried to teach *me* a thing or two about bed artistry. Can you believe that – my own sister! Some crackpot idea about saving me from my friends . . .

Bernie laughs.

> . . . She's a sick twist all right.

> TOM
> She speaks highly of you.

Bernie shrugs.

> BERNIE
> Yeah, well, you stick by your family. The point is, I can help you with your debts if that would make us friends. My motto is, a guy can't have too many. Big payday Saturday, Tom. You could be in on it.

For the first time, Tom is interested.

> TOM
> Another fix? Which fight?

175

BERNIE

Well, that's confidential at the moment. But it doesn't have to stay that way.

Tom gives Bernie a speculative eye.

TOM

How d'you know about it? Caspar isn't laying any more bets with you.

BERNIE

Mm.

Tom smiles humorlessly.

TOM

. . . You must have Mink jumping through hoops.

Bernie gets to his feet, wiping the knife blade on his coat.

BERNIE

Like I say, you can't have too many.

He goes to the door, looks up and down the hall, and turns back to Tom.

. . . We got a deal?

TOM

. . . I'll think about it.

On his way out:

BERNIE

I wouldn't want it any other way.

STREET – DAY

Pulling Tom along the sidewalk.

TOM

Cud . . .

He is calling to a short rail-like man lounging against a building who joins him as he walks. CUD's *features are small and sharp except for one cheek, which is hugely distended by a wad of chewing tobacco.*

. . . My credit still good with you?

Cud gives a so-so flutter of his hand.

. . . Give me a hundred across on Tailor Maid in the third tonight.

Cud shakes his head.

                            CUD
Lazarre won't like it.

                            TOM
Try fifty across.

Cud shrugs.

                            CUD
I'll try. That'll make another one-fifty you owe him.

                            TOM
Only if I lose, Cud.

                            CUD
Tommy, the way you're goin' — horses got knees?

                            TOM
I dunno. Fetlocks.

                            CUD
Well, the way you're goin', if I was a horse I'd be down on my fetlocks prayin' you don't bet on me.

A huge man has walked up to flank Tom's other side. This is
FRANKIE. *He addresses Cud:*

                          FRANKIE
Drift, small guy.

                            CUD
Drop dead, ape.

                          FRANKIE
C'mon Tom, my boss wants to see you. He didn't have time to engrave nothin' formal.

Cud starts to fade away.

177

CUD
I'll see you later, Tommy. I gotta go spit.

CASPAR'S CARD ROOM – LATE AFTERNOON

It is a big place, a derelict room off the main floor of a club, containing a couple of card tables, straight-backed chairs, a ratty sofa.

At the cut we are tracking behind Tom as Frankie and TIC-TAC, *a small ferret-faced man, escort him into the room. We hear a woman speaking rapid-fire Italian.*

Sitting at one of the card tables is Caspar. With him is HIS WIFE, *a short, round Italian woman, and his son,* JOHNNY JR. *Johnny Jr., about five years old, is also very round. He wears a suit with short pants that show dimpled knees.*

Eddie Dane is sitting on the sofa, wearing his overcoat and his hat pushed back on his forehead. He watches the domestic scene without any particular warmth.

Caspar cuts his wife's speech short:

CASPAR
Whaddya mean he's eatin' too much? Whadduz the goddamn doctor know?

He turns to the little boy.

. . . What you eat for lunch?

JOHNNY JR.
A hot dog.

CASPAR
Just a hot dog?

JOHNNY JR.
A hot dog and mustard.

Caspar roars with laughter.

CASPAR
A hot dog and mustard! A hot dog and mustard! You hear that, Eddie! The kid's as smart as a whip! Even Uncle Eddie thinks that's funny.

178

The Dane's face remains a solemn mask.

. . . Whadduz the goddamn doctor know!

Caspar wipes away tears of mirth and digs in his pocket with his left hand. He extends two closed fists toward the boy:

. . . G'head, which hand is the penny in?

The boy touches his right fist.

. . . Choose again.

The boy just looks at him. Caspar scowls.

. . . Okay, here ya go. Take the penny. Shiny new penny.

To his wife:

. . . Take the kid. Wait in the car. Give'm a penny, boys.

Tic-Tac and Frankie dig in their pockets.

FRANKIE

I ain't got a penny, boss.

Caspar has turned his attention to a checkbook that lies on the table in front of him. As he writes:

CASPAR

Ah, well, that's a penny ya owe him. 'Lo Tom, what's the rumpus? You like kids?

TOM

No.

CASPAR
(absently)

Uh-huh. Have a seat. G'head.

He tears out the check.

. . . Well, you're missin' out on a complete life. I know, kids, big deal, but still, I'm tellin' ya . . .

He blows on the check.

. . . Anyway. Thanks for comin' by. I just wrote this check out to your bookmaker, Lazarre. It's for an even

fifteen hundred, which is more than I hear you owe him,
but I figure you can always use some money on the cuff, a
high roller such as yaself wuddya say?

TOM

. . . Thanks.

Caspar laughs.

CASPAR

Always the yapper, huh? Well, you're welcome. You
wanna know why I'm putting you square with Lazarre?

180

TOM

Not particularly.

CASPAR

Bad feeling. It's a poison, kid. I want everybody to be
friends. I do this, you're friends with Lazarre, he's friends
with you, and you're friends with me. And all you gotta
do, show you're a friend, is give me Bernie Bernbaum.
You know it's the right thing anyway; I can't keep any
discipline if I can't punish the people I need to punish.
The Shmatte steals from me, I can't have Leo givin' him a
shiny new penny. You find some way to make Leo
understand that.

TOM

So the deal is, I give you the Shmatte, smoothe it over
with Leo, and you bail me out with Lazarre.

CASPAR

Yeah, then we're all friends again: you, me, Leo, the
Dane.

Eddie Dane sneers from the couch:

DANE

We can maybe have tea sometime.

CASPAR

C'mon, Eddie. Friends is a mental state. Wuddya say, kid?

TOM

. . . I'll think about it.

CASPAR

He'll think about it. Hear that, Dane? That's terrific. The
kid's a thinker.

DANE

Does he want a pillow for his head?

CASPAR

Okay kid, think about it. It's a mental state. But if it'll
help you think, you should know that if you don't do this,
you won't be in any shape to walk out a here.

Tom considers this.

TOM

. . . Would that be physically, or just a mental state?

Caspar stares at him, then slowly tears up the check.

CASPAR

That ain't friendly, kid. I make you a nice offer, I get the high hat.

He gets up and walks to the door. Tic-Tac opens it for him and precedes him out.

Before following Caspar out the door, Eddie Dane grins at Tom.

DANE

Too bad for you, smart guy.

He leaves, shutting the door.

The room is quiet.

Tom looks at Frankie, the large man who has stayed behind.

After dully returning Tom's stare, Frankie takes off his suit coat and hangs it carefully on a rack by the door.

He approaches Tom.

Tom rises.

TOM

Hold it.

Frankie complies. Tom shrugs off his coat. He folds it neatly and turns to lay it on his chair.

When he turns around again he is holding the chair and smashes it into Frankie's face.

Frankie staggers back. He reaches up to his nose and his hand comes away bloody.

FRANKIE

. . . Jesus, Tom.

Tom holds his chair at the ready.

Frankie looks at him for a moment, then goes to the door, opens it, and leaves, shutting it behind him.

The room is very quiet. Tom still holds the chair. After a long beat he starts to put it down.

The door opens and he quickly raises the chair again.

Tic-Tac, the little ferret-faced man, is striding into the room. Frankie, the gorilla, follows cautiously.

Tic-Tac reaches Tom and blocks his swing of the chair with a raised forearm. He wraps both arms around the chair and pulls it away from Tom. As Frankie circles Tom, Tic-Tac tosses the chair away.

Frankie, behind Tom now, wallops him in the small of the back. The blow sends him staggering toward Tic-Tac, who cracks him in the jaw.

Frankie grabs Tom's hair and yanks his head back as Tic-Tac works on his midsection. Tom's hands are reaching back to grope for Frankie.

Still holding his hair with one hand, Frankie cuffs Tom awkwardly on the side of the head. Tom staggers around and Tic-Tac, now behind him, also hits him on the side of the head.

Tom goes down. His head hits the floor with a thunk.

We are low-angle on the floor. Beyond Tom, in the background, we see the door to the room.

The door splinters in with a crash.

Tic-Tac, cropped low by our angle, walks up to Tom as blue uniforms stream into the room.

TIC-TAC
Just in the nick of time, huh?

He hops and delivers a walloping kick to the back of Tom's head. On the impact we cut to:

BLACK

Over black we hear the sound of running water.

183

FADE IN:
TOM

He gasps for air as his head is pulled out from under a running faucet.

The UNIFORMED POLICEMAN *who was holding him there and is now pulling him up, grins.*

> COP
> No harm done. Unless your friend broke his foot.

Tom is still woozy.

> TOM
> . . . Wuzzit . . . How long . . . Where am I?

> COP
> Johnny Caspar's pleasure dome, same as when you left us, about ten seconds ago.

He leads Tom by the arm across the card room. ANOTHER COP *has Frankie cuffed in a straight-backed chair and is taking roundhouse swings at him. He pauses, breathing heavily.*

> SECOND COP
> . . . 'Lo, Tom. Care to skin a knuckle on your playmate here?

> TOM
> No . . . thanks, Delahanty . . .

> SECOND COP
> Well, if you change your mind, we'll be interrogatin' for a while.

GAMBLING FLOOR

Tom and his escort emerge onto the casino floor.

> FIRST COP
> What was that party about, anyway?

> TOM
> We do this every weekend.

184

Blue uniforms are everywhere. Some are escorting slovenly patrons and tuxedoed employees to the exit; some wield axes on the gaming equipment; others are using nightsticks to smash the bottles behind the bar. Tom winces at this.

TOM

Jesus . . .

He takes a bottle and glass from a table as they walk by.

. . . What the hell is the matter with you people?

FIRST COP

Well, they said make it hurt—so we make it hurt.

EXT. CASPAR'S CLUB

A sign on the facade claims that the building houses SABBATINI'S ANTIQUES AND COLLECTIBLES.

Holding his bottle and glass, Tom weaves across the street toward O'Doole, the police chief, who leans against a squad car chewing a toothpick. He is the only person on the scene not in motion, as his uniformed men hustle other men and tarted-up women into paddy wagons.

TOM

Drink, O'Doole?

O'Doole does not look at Tom as they talk; he is glumly taking in the spectacle.

O'DOOLE

I'm on duty.

Tom pours himself a glass.

TOM

To Volstead . . .

He tosses it back.

. . . Any news on Rug?

O'DOOLE

Still dead, far as I know.

185

TOM

Get a slug out of him?

O'DOOLE

Yeah, a twenty-two. Listen, Tom, I'm just the chief
around here so don't bother telling me if you don't happen
to feel like it, but what the hell is Leo doing?

TOM

Ours is not to reason why, friend.

O'DOOLE

Balls. Look at this mess. Make him listen to you, Tom. It
ain't right, all this fuss over one sheeny. Let Caspar have
Bernie – Jesus, what's one Hebrew more or less?

He nods at the building.

. . . We're burning our meal ticket here.

TOM

Leo'll do what suits him and you'll do what he tells you.
Last I heard Leo's still running this town.

O'DOOLE

He won't be for long if this keeps up. It's no good for
anyone – you said as much yourself.

TOM

First off, O'Doole, I can say what I please to Leo and
about him . . .

He taps him on the chest.

. . . You can't. Second, once Leo decides – that's that.
And if that sticks going down, there are plenty of other
coppers wouldn't mind being chief, and could swallow it
clean.

O'Doole seems chastened.

O'DOOLE

Jesus, Tom, I was just speculatin' about a hypothesis. I
know I don't know nothin'. It's just a damn mess is all –

He is interrupted by gunfire from an upper story of the facing building. O'Doole's men react, finding cover, returning fire.

. . . a goddamn mess!

HALLWAY

We are over Tom's shoulder as he knocks at the door to Verna's apartment.

After a beat, Verna opens the door. On seeing who it is she starts to swing the door shut.

Tom puts his toe in the doorway and leans into the door. As he pushes his way in:

> TOM
>
> Thanks, don't mind if I do.

VERNA'S APARTMENT

She gives up and Tom enters.

Verna walks over to the phone. As she dials, Tom tosses his hat onto a chair and checks the apartment to see that they are alone.

> VERNA
>
> Hello, officer, I'd like to report an intruder at 346 West—

Tom grabs the phone away.

> TOM
>
> Who's this? . . . 'Lo, Shad, Tom Reagan here. We won't be needing any today . . . That's right, my mother. She didn't recognize me. Lemme talk to Mulvaney . . .

He takes out a flask and leers at Verna.

. . . Miss me?

> VERNA
>
> Drop dead.

We hear a voice barking through the line.

TOM

. . . 'Lo Sean, tell O'Doole to send a car over to Leo's tonight. If we're going to be banging away at Caspar, we ought to be ready for him to bang back . . . Yeah.

He cradles the phone and tips his flask back, draining it.

VERNA

What do you want?

Tom is crossing to the bar.

TOM

I was in the neighborhood, feeling a little daffy. Thought I'd drop in for an aperitif.

He pours himself a drink.

. . . Rug Daniels is dead.

VERNA

Gee, that's tough.

TOM

Don't get hysterical. I've had enough excitement for one night without a dame going all weepy on me.

VERNA

I barely knew the gentleman.

TOM

Rug? Bit of a shakedown artist. Not above the occasional grift, but you'd understand that. All in all, not a bad guy, if looks, brains, and personality don't count.

VERNA

You better hope they don't.

Tom gives her a sick grin.

TOM

Yeah, well, we're none of us the saint I hear your brother is.

VERNA

Who killed him?

TOM

Leo thinks Caspar did.

VERNA

But you know better.

TOM

I do now. Caspar just tried to buy me into settling his tiff
with Leo, which he'd hardly do if he was waging war. So I
figure you killed him, angel. You or Saint Bernard.

VERNA

Why would I – or my brother – kill Rug Daniels or
anybody else?

TOM

Rug was following you. He knew about you and me. That
wouldn't help your play with Leo, would it?

He looks at her. She holds his gaze.

VERNA

You think I murdered someone. Come on, Tom, you
know me a little.

TOM

Nobody knows anybody – not that well.

VERNA

You know or you wouldn't be here.

TOM

Not at all, sugar. I came to hear your side of the story –
how horrible Rug was, how he goaded you into it, how he
tried to shake you down –

VERNA

That's not why you came either.

Tom shrugs.

TOM

Tell me why I came.

VERNA

The oldest reason there is.

189

TOM

There are friendlier places to drink.

VERNA

Why can't you admit it?

TOM

Admit what?

VERNA

Admit you don't like me seeing Leo because you're jealous. Admit it isn't all cool calculation with you – that you've got a heart – even if it's small and feeble and you can't remember the last time you used it.

TOM

If I'd known we were going to cast our feelings into words, I'd have memorized the Song of Solomon.

Verna smiles.

VERNA

. . . Maybe that's why I like you, Tom. I've never met anyone made being a sonofabitch such a point of pride.

She turns to walk away.

. . . Though one day you'll pay a price for it.

Tom grabs her wrist.

TOM

Okay, Verna. But until then, let's get stinko.

He draws her close.

VERNA

. . . Let's do something else first.

She reaches up, takes off his hat, and tosses it away. We pan with the hat to where it lands on the floor, in front of a curtained window.

TOM (*off*)

Yeah. Let's do plenty.

190

DISSOLVE THROUGH TO:
ANOTHER WINDOW

It stands open, its white sheers billowing lazily in the draft.

Faintly, from another room in the house, we hear a phonograph recording of John McCormack singing "Danny Boy."

At the cut we hear a thump, close by, and briefly the sounds of a struggle. We then hear a breathy, gurgling sound, which quickly subsides.

The living room is late-night quiet.

A lateral track brings us off the window to an end table in the foreground. On the table is a pouch of Bull Durham, a package of rolling papers, a cup of coffee with steam rising off of it, and a section of a newspaper. The draft gently lifts a couple of rolling papers off the table.

The continuing track takes us off the end table and, booming down, shows us an upset chair and the legs of the man who occupied it.

We track along the man's body to discover that he is face-down on the section of newspaper he was reading, blood oozing out of his slit throat onto the paper.

The continuing track shows that, between the fingers of one outflung hand, a cigarette burns. It is resting on the newspaper.

We see the feet of another man who is turning from the man on the floor and walking away into the background. We pan over to watch him recede, framing out all of the dying man except for his outflung hand and cigarette.

As the walking man recedes, more and more of his topcoated body crops in. By the time he reaches the house's front door, in the deep background, we can see him full figure.

The newspaper in the foreground is crackling into flame. The rug it rests on is beginning to smoke and discolor.

As the man in the background opens the front door we jump in:

OVER HIS SHOULDER

Waiting in the darkness just outside is another man in a topcoat and fedora. He is holding two tommy guns.

The men do not exchange words.

The man outside hands his partner a tommy gun and follows him back into the house.

Still faint, we continue to hear "Danny Boy." We also hear the lick of flames.

A VICTROLA

The song is louder at the cut. We are in an upstairs bedroom.

LEO

Stretched out on his bed, wearing a robe over his pyjamas, smoking a cigar, listening—but only to the phonograph. Its sound covers any other noise in the house.

STAIRWAY

Close track on the two pairs of feet climbing the stairs. We see only the feet, the swaying hems of the topcoats, and, occasionally dipping into frame, the muzzles of the two tommy guns.

LEO'S BEDROOM

Leo is looking down, puzzled.

HIS POV

The floor.

Thin smoke sifts up through the floorboards.

HALLWAY

Tracking on the approaching feet. The song grows louder.

LEO'S BEDROOM

Leo slowly takes the cigar from his mouth.

BEDROOM DOOR

From inside as — CRASH — it is kicked in.

LEO

Hitting the floor and rolling under the bed.

THE TWO GUNMEN

Striding into the room.

LEO

On his belly under the bed, facing the door, swinging a handgun in front of him.

HIS POV

From floor level, the underside of the mattress above us, the floorboards stretching away.

The bed crops the two gunmen mid-shin. They swing their guns up, firing.

RAT-TAT-TAT-TAT — the hems of their coats sway as they fire.

The floorboards in front of us are pocked by bullets that walk across the floor toward the bed.

The mattress above us dances under the gunfire as ticking sprays down at the floor.

Smoke curls up through the floorboards.

LEO

Jaw clamped on his cigar, he fires.

HIS POV

Blood spurts as one gunman takes a hit in the ankle. He staggers and his tommy gun clatters to the floor.

LEO

Firing.

HIS POV

The other gunman is ducking out the door.

The injured gunman pitches forward, head toward us, his hat rolling away.

LEO

Firing.

HIS POV

A bullet opens the top of the fallen man's head.

LEO

Rolling out from under the bed.

He stoops to pick up the dead man's tommy gun. Thick smoke seeps up through the floor.

The phonograph plays.

Leo ducks out the door.

HALLWAY

We are looking down the length of the dark hall.

Leo crosses frame in the foreground to enter a facing room, as muzzle flashes erupt at the end of the hall—where the other gunman has been waiting in the darkness.

SECOND ROOM

Leo throws open a window.

EXTERIOR

Leo rolls out onto the long sloping eave of a front porch.

His gun skates down the eave and falls. Leo grabs the rain gutter, hangs by his hands, and drops down to the front lawn.

The first floor of the house is in flames.

We crane down on Leo as he picks up the gun and backs away from the house, looking up at the second story. His open robe flaps in the breeze. The dead cigar is still clamped between his teeth.

HIS POV

Staccato gunfire erupts in the dark second-story room Leo just exited.

The strobing gunfire makes a strobing shadow of the gunman, whose back is to us as he rakes the room with fire.

LEO

Firing, the gun jumping and bucking in his hands.

THROUGH THE WINDOW

The gunman, riddled with bullets and showered with broken glass, spins around, spastically firing his own Thompson.

Bullets dance across the walls and ceiling, blast out the remaining glass, and sing harmlessly into the trees outside.

BACK TO LEO

We hear the screech of skidding tires. A black coupe takes a curve on the street behind him, machine gun fire spitting from its back window.

Leo turns in the glow of the flames and walks calmly into the street, firing at the receding car.

THE CAR

Growing smaller, spitting fire and lead.

PULLING LEO

Still walking calmly up the street, the gun still bucking in his hands. Bullets whistle by and claw up the pavement around him.

BEHIND LEO

His robe whips back in the breeze. He fires again and we hear the distant sound of shattering glass.

The car weaves, runs up off the road, hits a tree, and bursts into flame.

A figure emerges from the car and staggers off into the darkness. The man is on fire.

LEO

He stops, squinting.

HIS POV

The burning gunman zig-zags into the darkness.

BACK TO LEO

A faint smile curls around the cigar. He drops the muzzle of the gun.

                              LEO
    Hunh . . .

The car explodes in a fireball as we cut to:

HALLWAY

The explosion echoes over the cut as we track up the hall pulling Tom and a tall cadaverous man with prematurely white hair. This is DEAD TERRY MCGILL.

Gunmen of every description line the hallway, lounging against the walls.

                              TOM
    Who's winning?

                             TERRY
    We are, for the nonce.

                              TOM
    What's the disposish?

                             TERRY
    Last night? Four to one. Dana Cudahy went up with the
    house.

                              TOM
    And theirs?

                             TERRY
    One burned.

                              TOM
    The other three?

                             TERRY
    Lead.

                              TOM
    Whose?

                             TERRY
    Leo's.

He is opening the door to admit Tom. In a voice low with admiration:

. . . The old man's still an artist with a Thompson.

LEO'S OFFICE

As Tom enters, Leo is bellowing into the phone:

LEO

—Well find him, goddamnit! Go see if he fell in the john!

He slams down the phone.

. . . Sonofabitch! No chief! Who's running the goddamned store?

Tom goes to the bar to pour himself a drink.

TOM

Can't raise O'Doole?

LEO

No, nor the mayor either.

TOM

Hmm.

He takes a sip.

. . . That's not good. They're running.

LEO

They wouldn't dare.

TOM

I don't know, Leo. I warned you not to hit Caspar's club—

LEO

I'm still here, ain't I?

TOM

Caspar's play hurt you anyway.

LEO

Hah! That sorry sonofabitch just slit his own throat. He just made me decide to step on him—

TOM

Listen to me, Leo. Last night made you look vulnerable.
You don't hold elected office in this town. You run it
because people think you run it. Once they stop thinking
it, you stop running it.

LEO

Jesus, Tom, sounds like a bad break for me I wasn't killed.

TOM

I mean it, Leo. Start taking Caspar seriously.

LEO

Don't sing me the blues again, Tommy. I need your help.
He shoots, we gotta answer –

TOM

That's what got you in this mess.

LEO

I know, I know. Retreat to win. Give up Bernie. That'll
solve all our problems.

TOM

It won't anymore, I'll grant that. Now it's either you or
Caspar. But going toe-to-toe with a psychopath'll get you
nowhere. It'll force everyone to choose sides just when
you're looking shaky.

LEO

The hell I do!

TOM

Then where's the mayor? Why aren't there any police
here? Why weren't there police at your place last night?

LEO

I didn't ask for any.

TOM

I did.

Leo chuckles.

LEO

Mother hen, huh? What's the matter, Tommy, you think I can't take care of myself?

TOM

I *know* you can't. Here's the smart play, Leo: you lay back, give up Bernie, let Caspar think he's made his point. Wait for him to show you a weakness –

LEO

Please, Tom . . .

Tom stares at him.

TOM

You're sticking on Bernie. Sticking your neck out for a guy who'd chop *you* off at the heels if there was two bits in it.

Leo leans back in his chair, puts his feet up, and gazes out the window.

LEO

. . . Tom, it ain't all as clear-cut as you make it . . . Bernie's – well hell, you know about me and Verna . . . Things now are – not that I haven't been a gentleman, but . . . I, uh . . . I plan to ask her to marry me, Tom.

There is a long beat. Leo avoids Tom's look, but finally responds to the silence:

. . . I guess you think that's a bonehead play.

TOM

Do you think she wants you to?

LEO

How the hell do I know, Tom? I think she does. – Yeah, 'course she does. I know, I know, you think different but – well, we just differ on that.

TOM

Leo . . .

Tom takes a deep breath.

201

. . . Caspar didn't kill Rug.

LEO
(absently)
Course he did.

TOM
No. Think about it. Just this one time. Who was Rug following?

This gets Leo's attention. He turns to look at Tom.

LEO
. . . Huh?

TOM
It needn't have been that sinister. A strange man, following her down a dark alley, late at night – I've told you, Leo, she can take care of herself.

Leo stares at Tom, dazed.

LEO
. . . Tom, why're you saying that? Christ, Tom. I just told you, I plan to –

TOM
They pulled a twenty-two slug out of him. A pop gun, Leo – a woman's gun.

LEO
. . . That's a whiskey dream. Verna wouldn't panic – shoot someone – just because he was following her . . .

He gazes off again, shaking his head.

. . . No . . . It wouldn't have happened that way in the first place, and if it had she would have told me . . . I know you don't like her, Tom, but I trust Verna as much as I trust you.

TOM
On her account you'll burn the town down.

                              LEO
Don't worry, Tom. We'll still be standing when the smoke
clears.

                              TOM
Okay, Leo. Then maybe it wasn't that innocent. Maybe
Rug knew something she didn't like him knowing, and
wouldn't want you to know. He was following her. He
knew who she was seeing. He knew where she was
sleeping, and who with . . .

*Leo has taken his feet off the sill and has turned back to face
Tom. He studies him carefully.*

                              LEO
Maybes don't make it so.

                              TOM
They're more than maybes. You've trusted me before, and
never lost anything by it. Trust me on this.

                              LEO
This is too important.

                              TOM
I don't ask much, and I don't ask often. Trust me on this.

                              LEO
Tommy—

                              TOM
Trust me on this or the hell with you.

                              LEO
You don't mean that.

                              TOM
. . . She was at my place. The night Rug was following
her, the night you dropped by.

Leo stares at Tom. Tom stares back.

*After a long beat Leo slowly rises, walks over to the window,
shoves his hands in his pockets, and gazes out.*

                              203

For a moment Tom looks at Leo's motionless back. Then he rises, plucks his hat from the desk, and goes to the door. Before exiting, he looks back.

Leo, in long shot, is still gazing out the window.

Tom exits.

HALLWAY

We pull Tom up the hall.

Behind him we see the door to Leo's office opening and Leo emerging. He strides up the hall after Tom.

Tom turns as Leo reaches him.

Leo, without breaking stride, walks right into him, throwing a punch that catches Tom on the chin and sends him stumbling back, his hat flying off.

The men lining the hall watch with casual interest.

Tom staggers into one of the men, who catches him. Another man has picked up Tom's hat and now hands it to him. The first man shoves Tom back into the middle of the hall just in time for the approaching Leo to land another punch against his jaw.

This blow sends Tom rolling down the stairs at the end of the hall, still clutching his hat.

Leo clomps down the stairs; his army of private retainers clomps down behind him. In his shirtsleeves and chomping an unlit cigar, Leo looks like a labor leader taking the rank and file to the barricades.

Tom claws himself to his feet.

Leo has reached the floor and still without breaking stride uppercuts Tom with a blow that straightens him and sends him staggering like a drunk into gamblers in evening dresses and tuxedos.

A path clears for Leo and his entourage. Tom weaves, watching Leo approach, but makes no attempt to defend himself.

Leo grabs his own wrist with one hand and swings his elbow up to catch Tom with a sharp blow to the side of his face.

Tom spins into a SCREAMING LADY *in a sequined evening dress and sinks to the floor, grabbing at her bodice and skirt for support. She bats at him with her handbag.*

Fat Tony emerges from the crowd and helps Tom to his feet. He raises a hand to stop Leo.

TONY
Okay, Leo. I'll throw him out.

Leo stops, panting. He is looking at Tom, but speaking to Tony:

LEO
. . . Yeah. Do that. It's the kiss-off. If I never see him again it'll be soon enough.

TOM'S APARTMENT

Wide shot of the living room, facing the windows. It is night.

Tom sits with his back to us at the window, feet propped up on the sill. He is smoking a cigarette. A full ashtray at his side suggests that he has been sitting there for some time.

We are tracking slowly in.

After a moment he stubs out his cigarette, picks up the phone, and dials.

TOM
. . . 'Lo Frankie, it's Tom, how's the flunky business? . . . I've had worse; your ventilator mending? . . .

Offscreen we hear a knocking at the front door. Tom ignores it.

. . . Tell Caspar it's already forgotten. I'd like to see him . . .

The knocking continues.

. . . All right, let me know.

He cradles the phone, lights another cigarette, takes a drag, and blows a thoughtful cloud of smoke. After a beat he rises and leaves frame.

THE DOOR

As Tom swings it open. Verna stands in the hallway. After a wordless beat she moves past him into the apartment. Tom turns and follows her.

He goes to the bar, pours two drinks, crosses to Verna, who has seated herself, hands her a drink, and sits in a chair facing hers.

VERNA

. . . It worked, whatever you did; Leo told me we're quits. But you know I didn't have anything to do with Rug.

TOM

Maybe not. Anyway, that isn't what soured him on you.

The thought is bitter, but her tone isn't:

VERNA

Oh, you and me, huh? You always take the long way around to get what you want, don't you, Tom. You could have just asked.

Tom looks at her.

TOM

. . . What *did* I want?

Verna returns his look.

VERNA

Me.

After a beat Tom brings the glass to his lips. The ice cubes clink.

FADE OUT

FADE IN:

TOM'S BEDROOM

Tom sits perched on the edge of the bed, smoking a cigarette. Verna is in bed behind him. The lamp on the nightstand burns a faint yellow.

The telephone rings.

As Tom reaches for it, Verna stirs.

TOM

Yeah?

He reaches over to switch off the light. When he does the room remains illuminated by dull gray light; it is dawn.

. . . Yeah, yeah, when? . . . Okay.

He hangs up and continues to smoke, staring absently off.

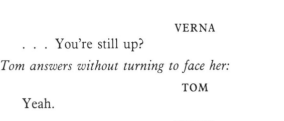

VERNA

. . . You're still up?

Tom answers without turning to face her:

TOM

Yeah.

VERNA

. . . What're you chewing over?

TOM

. . . Dream I had once. I was walking in the woods, don't know why. The wind came up and blew my hat off—

VERNA

And you chased it, right? You ran and ran and finally you caught up to it but it wasn't a hat anymore. It had changed into something else—something wonderful.

TOM

No. It stayed a hat. And, no, I didn't chase it . . .

He draws on the cigarette.

. . . Nothing more foolish than a man chasing his hat.

Tom rouses himself, rises, and we pan to follow him as he picks up a shirt and starts buttoning it in the bureau mirror.

VERNA

Where're you going?

TOM

Out.

VERNA

Don't let on more than you have to.

Tom shrugs.

TOM

Just have to do a few things.

VERNA

. . . You and Leo might still be able to patch things up.

Tom grimaces.

208

TOM

Me and Leo are finished. Nothing's going to change that.

VERNA

You never know. He's got a big heart.

TOM

We're quits—as far as I'm concerned, never mind him.
And if Leo *did* want me back, he's an even bigger sap than
I thought.

VERNA

Then why don't we just pick up and leave town? There's
nothing keeping you here. I know there's nothing keeping
me.

Tom is starting to knot a tie.

TOM

What about Bernie?

VERNA

He could come with us.

TOM

You, me, and Bernie. Where would we go, Verna—
Niagara Falls?

VERNA

Why do you hate him?

TOM

I don't hate anyone.

VERNA

Or like anyone.

TOM

Whatever. Where *is* Bernie?

Verna looks at him.

VERNA

Why?

TOM

Leo can't protect him anymore. I ought to tell him to skip.

VERNA

The Royale. Room 302.

She gazes off.

. . . I guess we both double-crossed Leo, there's no getting around that. I guess he's well rid of both of us.

TOM

Mm.

VERNA

The two of us, we're about bad enough to deserve each other.

TOM

Are we?

VERNA

We're a couple of heels, Tom. Yes, we are.

CASPAR'S OFFICE – DAY

We are pulling Tom into the office. Behind him, Frankie, his nose swathed in bandages, closes the door from the outside.

CASPAR (*off*)

'Lo, kid. You know O'Doole . . .

REVERSE

Caspar sits behind his desk. Eddie Dane sits slouched on a sofa to one side, wearing his hat, his hands jammed into the pockets of his overcoat.

In two chairs facing the desk sit two familiar men who are twisting around to smile at Tom.

CASPAR

. . . and the mayor.

TOM

'Lo, boys.

                    MAYOR
Tom's a big booster. Always has been.

                    CASPAR
S'fine, s'fine. Well, Tom and me's got the proverbial fat to
chew—

The mayor and O'Doole get to their feet.

                    MAYOR
Well, let us know if you need anything.

                    CASPAR
Yeah, happy days. Have a seat, kid . . .

Tom sits into one of the vacated chairs.

    . . . So, you had enough time to think about things?

                    TOM
Yeah, well, circumstances have changed.

                    CASPAR
Don't I know it. Last night I know the Dane was
disappointed the bulls showed up before Frankie and Tic-
Tac could really pin your ears back, but I said, relax,
Eddie, I got a feeling about this kid. Take the long view.
The kid and Leo are gonna go bust-o. If the kid ain't
ready yet, well, he soon will be. Matter of time. I said, the
kid's too smart for Leo—that's what I said. Like a psychic.
Ask the Dane if I didn't. Like a goddamn psychic. G'head.
Ask him.

Tom turns to the Dane.

                    TOM
You vouch for this psychic business?

                    DANE
That's right, smart guy.

*Caspar, oblivious to any hostility in the room, cheerfully
continues.*

CASPAR

I know you knew protecting the Shmatte was a dumb idea.
I know you been wise to all of Leo's dumb ideas lately.
Only a matter of time. Bust-o.

He chuckles.

. . . That's why last night we didn't put the arm on you.
Only Leo.

TOM

Seeing how you squiffed your play on Leo, I can be only
so grateful.

DANE

That's brave, coming from Little Miss Punching Bag.

CASPAR

C'mon Eddie. Friends now, huh?

DANE

Nuts.

Caspar smiles at Tom.

212

CASPAR
So I guess you're looking for a job, huh, kid?

TOM
I might be.

Caspar laughs.

CASPAR
You got references? You been to college, kid? We only take yeggs what's been to college. Ain't that right, Dane?

The Dane's scowl is set in cement.

. . . I'm jokin', of course. We all know you can be useful to us, a smart kid such as yaself, the man who walks behind the man and whispers in his ear. I guess you could be useful, in spades.

TOM
Yeah. I can do plenty for you. But can you keep Leo off me?

CASPAR
I'm tellin' ya not to worry about Leo. We got plans for him.

TOM
Yeah? What?

DANE
Not so fast there, Kaputnik.

There is a beat through which Caspar continues to smile at Tom.

CASPAR
. . . I think what the Dane is trying to say is, there'll be time to talk about that. That can be tabled for a later date. See, the last time we jawed you gave me the high hat. So I guess I'm sayin', maybe we want your confidence before we give you ours. You gotta put somethin' on the table first. Ante up.

TOM
Fair enough. Where shall we start?

CASPAR

Hear that, Eddie? All business! I told you he was a good kid! Where shall we start! All business!

He rocks back in his chair, laughing. Tom smiles pleasantly. Finally Caspar sighs.

 . . . Well, we could start for instance with the Shmatte, like where's the Shmatte? You could maybe tell us that.

TOM

The Royale. Room 302. And you might find Mink with him.

DANE

The hell you say.

TOM

Sure, Bernie and Mink are as cozy as lice.

He turns to look at the Dane.

 . . . And it ain't just business.

Caspar looks at the Dane, who glares at Tom.

DANE

This guy's lying.

Tom shrugs.

TOM

Why would I? .

DANE

This guy's wrong. This guy's all wrong. Mink is clean and this clown is a smart guy.

Caspar is still staring at the Dane, no longer smiling.

CASPAR

Easy enough to find out, ain't it? You find Mink, bring him back here.

He nods at Tom

 . . . You go down to the car. I'll send Frankie and Tic-

Tac with you to the Royale. If Bernie's there, Frankie and Tic-Tac'll take care of him.

                              DANE
And if he's not there?

Tom shrugs.

                              TOM
I'll sit facing the corner in a funny hat.

EXT.   THE ROYALE

Tom sits behind the wheel of a parked car. We are on his rigidly set profile.

BAM—*Bernie Bernbaum's face is slammed against the driver's window. Tom does not react.*

Bernie is wailing as he is muscled away by two topcoated figures whose faces are cropped by the car window.

They shove Bernie out of frame toward the rear of the car and we hear its back door being opened.

Bernie's voice, off, is near hysteria:

                              BERNIE
Frankie, let me go, I'm prayin' to ya, Jesus God—Tom! Jesus!

We hold on Tom's face as Frankie and Tic-Tac pile Bernie into the back.

. . . Are you part of this?! You can't be part of this! I think these guys're gonna whack me! You gotta talk to 'em, Tommy!

                              FRANKIE
You gimme a headache, you little sheeny.

To Tom:

                              TIC-TAC
Okay, we're going to Miller's Crossing.

Tom still does not react.

. . . Let's go!

As Tom reaches forward and starts the car:

BERNIE

You're not part of this! Tom! Help me! These guys are gonna whack me!

TIC-TAC

Whack you inna mouth you don't shut up.

MILLER'S CROSSING

A wooded area outside of town. The wind blows.

The car pulls into frame and stops on the shoulder. The backseat passengers—Frankie, Tic-Tac, and Bernie—emerge; Tom remains in the driver's seat.

Bernie is weeping, loudly. Frankie takes out a gun and whacks him smartly on the side of the head. The blow sends him stumbling over toward Tic-Tac, who kicks him down.

The blows haven't quelled Bernie's sobbing.

TIC-TAC

I don't want you runnin' anywhere.

Frankie takes a swig from his flask and hands it to Tic-Tac, who leans in the car window.

INT. CAR

Tom gazes forward, jaw set, eyes off the doings outside.

As Tic-Tac hands his gun in through the window:

TIC-TAC

Okay. Take him in the woods and whack him.

TOM

Huh? I don't . . .

216

Yeah, that's right, the boss wants you to do it. Make sure you're with the good guys.

Tom stares dumbly at the gun. Tic-Tac holds it, grip out toward him, motionless.

After a beat Tom takes the gun.

TIC-TAC
You know how to do this, right? You gotta remember to put one in his brain. Your first shot puts him down, then you put one in his brain. Then he's dead, then we go home.

Tom opens his door.

WIDE

Bernie is still on the ground, sobbing, as Frankie prods him with his foot.

FRANKIE
Get up.

BERNIE
I can't get up! I can't get up!

Frankie drags him to his feet.

FRANKIE
Get up and walk, you chiselin' little yid.

He pushes him toward the woods and reaches for the whiskey flask.

Bernie stumbles off; Tom follows.

TRACK

Through the woods, pulling the two men, Bernie leading. Tree limbs groan in the wind.

Bernie is stumbling, his clothes rumpled and dirty, his face stained by tears and blood from the gun blow. His shaking voice strains for a tone of reasonableness:

217

BERNIE

– Tommy, you can't do this. You don't bump guys.
You're not like those animals back there . . .

Tom marches on, face drawn, silent.

. . . It's not right, Tom. They can't make us do this. It's
a wrong situation. They can't make us different people
than we are. We're not muscle, Tom. I never killed
anybody. I used a little information for a chisel, that's all.
I couldn't help it, Tom, it's my nature. Somebody hands
me an angle, I play it. I don't deserve to die for that!
D'you think I do? I'm just a grifter! Huh, Tom? I'm
nobody!

*Still no response from Tom. Bernie fights a losing battle to keep
himself from whining.*

. . . But I'll tell you what, I never crossed a friend. Huh,
Tom? Never killed anybody, never crossed a friend. Nor
you, I'll bet. We're not like those animals. You can't *do*
this! You're not like those animals! This is not us! This is
some hop dream!

Bernie starts to weep.

. . . It's a dream! Tommy! I'm praying to you! I can't die!
I *can't* die! Out here in the woods! Like a dumb animal! I
can't die!

*He turns and sinks to his knees, wailing, his hands clasped in
front of him.*

. . . You *can't* kill me. I'm praying to you! Look in your
heart! I'm praying to you! Look in your heart!

Tom stares down at Bernie.

. . . I'm praying to you! Look in your heart!

Slowly Tom raises the gun and levels it at Bernie's head.

. . . Look in your heart! Look in your–

BOOM! *The gun blast is deafening. With it, Bernie's sobbing
abruptly stops.*

218

The shot echoes away in the woods, taking the wind with it, leaving silence.

CLOSE   BERNIE

Still kneeling, staring wide-eyed at Tom.

Finally he whispers:

> BERNIE
>
> . . . Tommy.

> TOM
>
> Shut up. You're dead, get me?

> BERNIE
>
> I understand. I'm dead. God bless you—

> TOM
>
> Shut up. You have to disappear. You have to blow for good. No one can see you, no one can know.

BERNIE

God bless you—

TOM

Go somewhere no one knows you. Anyone sees you, you really are dead, I don't care, you're not my problem any more.

BERNIE

Of course not. Of course not. You've done your share. Thank you. Don't worry, I understand. Thank you—

TOM

Shut up. Just get the hell out, before I change my mind.

Bernie is already on his feet and running.

CLOSE ON TOM

Watching Bernie go.

TRACKING

Pulling Bernie as he runs. Foreground trees flash by. In the background we see Tom standing, his gun held limply at his side.

Boom!—another gun blast. Running, Bernie reacts, but Tom has only fired into the ground.

On the echo of the shot we cut to:

THE ROAD

Tic-Tac and Frankie are leaning against the car, trading the flask back and forth.

Tom emerges from the woods.

FRANKIE

Put one in his brain?

Tom takes a few steps more before answering:

TOM

. . . Yeah.

FRANKIE

Attaboy.

FADE OUT

Over black we hear the sound of coins being dropped into a phone box.

FADE IN

PHONE BOOTH – DESERTED STREET – NIGHT

An extreme wide shot of Tom, who stands inside the distant booth, waiting, the receiver to his ear.

TOM

Mink? Tom Reagan. Where've you been? . . .

CLOSE ON TOM

Hunched, his back to us.

TOM

. . . Well you're lucky, Eddie Dane's been looking for you. Bernie's dead – stop wailing and listen to me. Caspar knows you were in on selling out his fix . . . I guess *I* gave him that idea. Sorry, Mink, we were chatting and it just slipped out. – Shut up and let me talk. You've gotta lay low till Caspar cools off, then you're gonna tell him Eddie Dane put you up to it. Tell him the Dane was behind the sell-out and I'll make Caspar go easy on you . . . That's right, I got you into this. Just remember, Mink, I'm the only one who can get you out.

Tom hangs up the phone, turns around, and opens the glass door.

WHOMMMP! *A fist slams into his stomach, driving him back into the phone booth, knocking his hat off of his head.*

The hat is picked up, dusted off, and handed back into the booth. It is Dead Terry, the tall cadaverous man we saw earlier outside of Leo's office. A cigarette dangles from his lower lip.

221

Behind him, a black sedan is parked at the curb. Three or four gunmen stand on the sidewalk looking warily up and down the street.

Tom reaches feebly out for his hat.

> TOM
>
> 'Lo, Terry. Getting out the vote?

Dead Terry flicks away his cigarette and smiles.

> TERRY
>
> Message from Leo. Leo says, if you're smart you'll sit this one out – not that he cares one way or the other. Leo says if you're on the wrong side you take your chances, like anyone else. Leo says he gives no special favors. That's all.

> TOM
>
> Mm . . .

Terry starts to turn away.

> . . . Tell Leo he's not God on the throne, he's just a cheap mick political boss with more hair tonic than brains.

Tom moves to exit the booth, but Terry lays a hand on his shoulder.

> TERRY
>
> One more thing . .

He cracks Tom across the chin with a clean left hook, knocking him back into the booth.

Tom rubs his chin, looking up at Terry.

> TOM
>
> Leo say that too?

As Terry and the gunmen get into the car:

> TERRY
>
> No, I said that. Cross Leo and next time I'll say plenty.

We fade out as the door slams and the car roars off.

Over black we hear:

222

CASPAR

When you're right you're right, but you never say I told
you so.

FADE IN

On Tom, sitting into frame in Caspar's office.

TOM

So what'm I right about?

Behind his desk, Caspar smiles.

CASPAR

Well, I'll tell ya, but first you gotta promise not to say I
told you so.

Tom takes out a pack of cigarettes.

TOM

I never say that. And I don't like people who do.

CASPAR

Mink was robbin' me right along with the Shmatte.

TOM

. . . What convinced you of that?

CASPAR

Mink Larouie took a powder. We can't find him. The
Dane's makin' excuses for him, but personally, I think you
were right. I think Mink and Bernie was in it together. I
think Mink heard you'd bumped the Shmatte and lit out –
the lousy sonofabitch!

*His eyes on Caspar, Tom takes out a cigarette, lights it, takes a
deep drag.*

TOM

. . . I told you so.

Caspar stares hard for a beat, then laughs.

CASPAR

Ogay. You got a lip on ya. At's all right. I don't generally care for it, but that's all right. You were a good sport to bump the Shmatte.

TOM

How d'you know Mink skipped?

CASPAR

The Dane can't find him.

TOM

So he says.

Caspar stares at Tom.

CASPAR

Meanin' what, exactly?

TOM

Maybe nothing. I didn't give it much thought until now, since a guy will say pretty much anything when he knows his number is up, but just before I bumped Bernie he swore to me that Mink and the Dane were setting him up. That they were the ones that were selling out your fix.

CASPAR

Zat so . . .

He looks at Tom.

. . . Like you say, a guy'll say anything.

TOM

Uh-huh. So why isn't Eddie Dane here?

CASPAR

Well . . .

He fidgets.

. . . He don't care for you, kid. Maybe it's only fair to tell you . . . After you left us, he tried to sell me on a double-cross. He says to me, why don't we double-cross you and give you the bump once we get the Shmatte. But I figure a deal's a deal, you're square with me, you bump

224

the Shmatte, I'll hold up my end. Question of ethics. Everything aboveboard, that's how I like it, so everybody knows who's a friend and who's an enemy. But the Dane wouldn't cross *me*. We go back.

                              TOM
Uh-huh. Course, there's always that wild card when love is involved.

                            CASPAR
. . . I know Mink is Eddie Dane's boy, but I still don't make it that way.

                              TOM
Mm. Well, then there's nothing to worry about.

Caspar is lost in thought.

                            CASPAR
Yeah . . .

We hear the door to the office open off screen and Johnny Jr. runs into frame clutching a scrolled piece of paper.

                         JOHNNY JR.
Poppa! Poppa! I got a prize from the—

Caspar holds up a hand to quiet the youngster.

                            CASPAR
Just a minute . . . Course, there's no reason not to be careful—

                         JOHNNY JR.
Poppa! Poppa! The sisters gave me a—unnh!

Caspar has cuffed him sharply on the side of the head. He points at Tom.

                            CASPAR
Shaddap! You take a page outta this guy's book. A little less you talk and a little more you think!

Caspar looks at Tom.

. . . Kids. Ya gotta be firm. Anyways. You know what I'm sayin'. No reason to worry but no reason not to investigate, neither. If Mink is around I want you to find him. He can tell us what's what . . .

To Johnny Jr.:

. . . What's a matter, somebody hit you, what's a matter, we ain't friends anymore? . . .

He picks up Johnny Jr., who is crying softly, and sets him on his lap. Encouraged by the attention, the child starts to wail. Caspar bounces him on his knee and raises his voice over the sobs:

. . . If you find him, I wanna talk to him alone. That's how you get the straight dope. Man-to-man. Just me, Mink . . .

He pats his jacket where his shoulder holster is.

. . . and my friend Roscoe. Y'understand what I'm sayin'?

Tom takes a contemplative drag on his cigarette.

TOM

. . . It ain't complicated.

CLOSE SHOT   A MAN'S FACE

Crunch! – being hit by a gloved hand.

The blow and the man's grunt echo.

CLOSE ON A NEWSPAPER

The sound of fists against flesh continues, echoing, in the background.

The newspaper headline reads: PARTY BOSS LOSES MUNICIPAL CONTRACT. *The subhead reads:* Liam "Leo" O'Bannon Removed From City Highway Commission. *Second subhead:* New Construction Contracts To Raffo Bros.

ON TOM

Leaning against a pillar in a large bare room with a hardwood floor. He is reading the newspaper.

226

We are in a gym. In a ring in the background two boxers are sparring as two or three old men with towels slung over their shoulders and elbows hooked over the ropes offer halfhearted advice.

We hear high heels echoing across the floor and Verna enters.

TOM

You should leave town for a few days; things are going to heat up here. Go out to the Palisades; I'll join you once I'm done –

VERNA

I can't find Bernie. Did you find him?

Tom looks out at the fighters in the background, avoiding Verna's look.

TOM

. . . Yeah.

VERNA

Is he leaving?

TOM

He left.

VERNA

Where to?

TOM

. . . He didn't say. You should –

She reaches out to touch his hand.

VERNA

Thanks.

She leans in to embrace him.

Tom's eyes drift up to the fighters.

EXT. THE GYM

Peeling paint on its blacked-out window reads: Gleason's Gym. Training in The Sweet Science.

Verna is exiting the gym in long shot.

We pull back to bring Eddie Dane into frame. He sits in the driver's seat of a car, watching Verna recede. He murmurs:

                              DANE
      What's he up to?

An offscreen voice, a passenger:

                              VOICE
      Beats me.

                              DANE
      That's Bernie's sister, isn't it?

                              VOICE
      Beats me.

                              DANE
      What's he seeing her for?

                              VOICE
      Beats me, maybe he's —

                              DANE
      Shut up. Get lost.

The Dane reaches for the ignition as we hear the car door open.

      . . . I'll see where the twist flops.

INT. SPEAKEASY

A hand swings through frame to smash a gun butt into a surprised face.

With a loud crash the surprised man stumbles back into a table and flops to the floor. He is round, aproned, middle-aged. Coat-skirted legs approach and start kicking at him.

The prostrate man rolls across the floor, trying to shield himself from the blows.

                        CLOSE VOICE
      C'mon, get up. I just wanna talk.

FAR VOICE

Yeah, get up. He ain't gonna hurt ya.

ROUND MAN

He already hurt me! He broke my goddamn nose!

ROOSTER, *the man standing over him, has a long scar across his neck and a rasping voice:*

ROOSTER

So what? I had my nose broke once.

ROUND MAN

I already paid Leo's men!

BERT, *another enforcer, is down at the end of the bar with Tom.*

BERT

You still pay Leo for protection? Is he protectin' you?

Rooster kicks at the little round man:

ROOSTER

We's protectin' you. Johnny Caspar's runnin' things or maybe you ain't heard.

Bert and Tom talk in the foreground as, in the background, Rooster continues to hector and kick at the round man.

TOM

So, the Dane hasn't got a line on Leo yet?

BERT

Not that I know about. He's been lookin', but I guess Leo's been movin' around and – hoist this over the bar, will ya? – things've been kinda hectic.

He is handing Tom a briefcase. Tom leans over the bar to drop it behind.

TOM

Do me a favor – let me know if he finds anything.

Bert pours himself a drink.

BERT

Yeah, okay.

Rooster, drawing his gun, calls from the back of the bar:

ROOSTER

I'm gonna put this one to sleep, wuddya think, Bert?

Bert shrugs into his overcoat.

BERT

Yeah, okay.

TOM

If you kill him, he won't be able to think things over.

ROOSTER

He don't seem like such a hot thinker.

TOM

You'll think about what you've learned here, won't you Louie?

ROUND MAN

You bet, Tom, I'll think plenty!

Bert shrugs clemency.

BERT

Ah, what the hell . . .

The round man scrambles to his feet and runs out the back door. Rooster puts away his gun and saunters over to Tom and Bert.

The three men head for the front door:

. . . If we can't trust a dago, the whole thing's hopeless anyway.

EXT. SPEAKEASY

The three men emerge into the afternoon sun.

TOM

So, we winning?

Bert gives a noncommittal shrug.

BERT

It's tough. Leo's still got some teeth left. His men
bushwhacked Tony Campisi last night, slit his t'roat.

ROOSTER

Yeah? He die?

BERT

I said, they slit his t'roat.

ROOSTER

So what, genius? I had my t'roat slit.

BERT

Sure, Rooster, but normal people's brains need oxygen.

BOOM!—*behind the three men the front of the speakeasy blows—
glass flying, flames licking out.*

*Though there is commotion among the passers-by, Tom, Bert, and
Rooster don't even turn to look.*

Get the car, will ya Rooster?

Rooster trots out into the street.

TOM

Don't tell the Dane I was asking about him.

BERT

Yeah, yeah.

TOM

Caspar just wanted me to check up, make sure he's doing
everything he can—

There is a faint but distinct popping sound.

Tom looks into the street.

*Rooster is staggering around as if drunk. He turns to face Tom
and Bert. He lurches toward them. A red stain is blossoming on
his chest.*

*The ambient hubbub fades to silence; we hear only the crisp
staggering scuffle of Rooster's shoes as he stumbles into the
foreground, looking stunned.*

He drops.
A woman screams.
Noise wells up.
Bert is unholstering his gun, looking up.
Tom looks where Bert is looking.

FACING ROOFTOP
*A man with a distinctive shock of white hair – Dead Terry
McGill – puts up his gun and starts running along the roof.*

BERT
*Starts running along the street to keep pace, firing up at the
facing roof.*

A POLICE CAR
*Siren wailing, up on two wheels as it takes a speeding turn onto
the street.*
It is hurtling toward Bert.

PULLING BERT
Running, pointing up, and bellowing at the oncoming car:
                              BERT
     Leo's man! Up there!

THE POLICE CAR
Cops with guns hang out every window. They start firing.

TRACKING TOWARD BERT
Running, pointing.

BERT
. . . Up there! Leo's—

Police bullets cut him to pieces. He hits the road, a limp rag.

The police car squeals to a halt in front of his corpse. A sergeant and his men tumble out.

Tom is sauntering over, smoking a cigarette.

SERGEANT
'Lo, Tom. Chalk one up for the good guys, huh?

TOM
Caspar'll be thrilled. You just shot one of his apes.

SERGEANT
Balls! That's Two-Toe Jackson!

Tom's attention is drawn by something down the street.

HIS POV

About a block away, a man with white hair is crossing the street.

SERGEANT (*off*)
I'm tellin' you that's Two-Toe Jackson! He's Leo's!

BACK TO TOM

As he leaves.

TOM
It's Bert Sachetti, Caspar's bang-man.

The sergeant bellows at another cop:

SERGEANT
Take his shoes off! Count his goddamn toes!

INT. DINER

Dead Terry McGill sits at a stool looking angrily down at a cup of coffee. Tom enters to sit next to him.

233

Through the windows behind them we see people running back and forth on the street, a fire engine racing past—furious activity, its noise muted inside the diner.

TOM

'Lo, Terry. You weren't aiming at me, were you?

Without looking up:

TERRY

In the first place, I don't know what you're talking about. In the second place, if I *had* been aiming at you I'd've hit you. In the third place, I don't know what you're talking about in the first place.

He tosses some coins onto the counter and gets up. We hold on Tom as Terry talks to Tom's back:

. . . I'd like to have, believe me. Leo won't let me—yet. But I'll bring him around.

He puts a hand on Tom's shoulder and swivels him around. Terry clenches a fist and draws it back to throw a punch.

Tom and Terry look at each other, Tom making no move to defend himself.

After a long beat, Terry unclenches his fist and sneers:

. . . I won't give you the satisfaction.

A DOORKNOB

As—CRASH—a foot enters to kick it and the door in.

VERNA'S APARTMENT

Verna is backing away; Eddie Dane strides into frame.

DANE

Know who I am?

Verna continues to back away; the Dane continues to advance.

VERNA

Yeah, Johnny Caspar's shadow. Did he stay in bed today?

DANE

Jesus. I open my mouth, the whole world turns
smart . . .

He glances around the room. Verna is backing around the couch.
The Dane continues to follow her.

. . . You're Leo's twist, right?

VERNA

Me and Leo are through.

She picks up her purse from the sill behind the couch and
rummages. Eddie Dane doesn't seem to mind.

DANE

Yeah? So you're sluttin' around with Tom now, huh?

Verna takes a gun from her purse and levels it at the Dane.

VERNA

Get outta here.

As he continues to walk toward her:

DANE

Okay, see ya later . . .

His hands flash — he has grabbed Verna's gun with one hand, her
arm with the other.

. . . Before I go, what's your boyfriend up to?

Verna struggles in his grasp, to no effect.

VERNA

Nothing I know about.

The Dane drags her close, nose to nose:

DANE

Yeah? It doesn't figure for me, your dumping Leo for the
guy who put a bullet in your brother.

Verna stops resisting and stares at him.

The Dane stares back, thinking.

. . . Didn't tell you, huh?

We hear a footstep.

Eddie Dane wheels, swinging Verna's body in front of his, as two topcoated figures enter, guns drawn.

FIRST GUNMAN

Spin her, Eddie!

Both intruders hold fire, their shot blocked by Verna. The gun in the Dane's hand barks once.

The lead man pitches forward, his gun clattering away.

His partner ducks back out the door.

Verna still struggles futilely; the Dane keeps his gun, peeking out from behind Verna, trained on the empty doorway.

The man on the floor, still alive, is clawing himself toward his gun, a few paces away.

The Dane ignores him. He watches the open door.

After a silent beat:

VOICE FROM HALL

. . . Let her go, Eddie, there's nothing you can do. Leave by the fire escape. There's more of us on the way—

BANG— *the Dane fires.*

Wood splinters in the door, which shudders back a few inches toward the wall. The voice from the hall has stopped short.

After a short silent beat, we hear a gun clatter to the hallway floor.

We hear fabric drag across wall, and then see the dead man drop to the floor just outside the door.

The Dane tosses Verna away and saunters unhurriedly over to the first man, who has almost reached his gun. Just as the man's hand closes over it the Dane, in stride, steps onto the hand and gun.

Head cocked, he looks down at the man in front of him.

DANE

You Leo's?

236

MAN

Yeah. He wanted her looked out for.

DANE

Well you did a bang-up job, I'll be sure to tell him. Where *is* Leo?

MAN

If I tell you, how do I know you won't kill me?

DANE

Because if you told me and I killed you and you were lying, then I wouldn't get to kill you then. Where's Leo?

MAN

. . . He's – he's moving around. But tomorrow night he's getting his mob together at Whiskey Nick's.

The Dane points his gun at the man's head.

DANE

You sure?

MAN

Check it. It's gold.

DANE

You know something, yegg? I believe you.

BANG.

The Dane turns from the body.

LOW AND WIDE ON THE DANE

One corpse on the floor beside him, the other corpse in the doorway behind him.

He absently wraps one hand around the warm barrel of the gun, then brings the hand up to blow against its open palm.

DANE

Go ahead and run, sweetie . . .

237

HIS POV   THE WINDOW

The main room is now empty. Sheers billow at the window, now open, that lets out on the fire escape. Off:

DANE
. . . I'll track down all a you whores.

DISSOLVE THROUGH TO:
ANOTHER WINDOW

Its sheers billow in the breeze.

TOM

Sitting in bed, smoking a cigarette, thinking. The bedroom is dark.

There is a knock at the apartment's front door. Tom reacts, but does not immediately rise.

The knock is repeated.

Tom finally swings his feet to the floor but the knocking stops and another sound brings him up short: The person at the door is now playing with the lock.

Tom sits motionless, listening.

After some rattling we hear the lock spring, then the door swinging open, then shutting again. We hear footsteps cross the main room, and then the squeak of chair springs.

Silence.

Tom smiles. He rises and walks to the living room doorway and leans against the jamb.

HIS POV

The windows throw moonlit squares onto the floor. We can see only the legs of someone sitting in the armchair.

TOM
'Lo, Bernie. Come on in, make yourself at home.

238

Bernie turns on the lamp on the table at his elbow. He holds a gun casually in his lap.

BERNIE

'Lo, Tom. Thought I'd do that, since you didn't seem to be in. Figured it was a bad idea to wait in the hall, seeing as I'm supposed to be dead.

TOM

Mm.

BERNIE

How'd you know it was me?

TOM

You're the only person I know'd knock and break in.

BERNIE

Your other friends wouldn't break in, huh?

TOM

My other friends wanna kill me, so they wouldn't knock.

He crosses to the chair facing Bernie's.

. . . What's on your mind, Bernie?

BERNIE

Things. I guess you must be kind of angry – I'm supposed to be gone, far away. I guess it seems sort of irresponsible, my being here . . .

Bernie leaves room for a response, but Tom is only listening.

. . . And I was *gonna* leave. Honest I was. But then I started thinking. If I stuck around, that would not be good for you. And then I started thinking that that might not be bad for me.

Tom still doesn't answer.

. . . I guess you didn't see the play you gave me. I mean, what'm I gonna do? If I leave, I got nothing – no money, no friends, nothing. If I stay, I got you. Anyone finds out I'm alive – you're dead, so . . . I got you, Tommy.

Tom is silent.

239

. . . What's the matter, you got nothin' to crack wise about? Bernie ain't so funny anymore?

Bernie's lip is quivering. His voice is softer:

. . . I guess I made kinda a fool a myself out there, bawling away like a twist. I guess . . .

His tone is bitter.

. . . I guess I turned yellow. — You didn't tell anyone about that?

TOM

No.

BERNIE

Course *you* know. It's a painful memory. And I can't help remembering that you put the finger on me, and you took me out there to whack me. I know you didn't . . . I know you didn't shoot me . . . but . . . but—

TOM

But what have I done for you lately?

BERNIE

Don't smart me.

He stares hard at Tom.

See, I wanna watch you squirm. I wanna see you sweat a little. And when you smart me, it ruins it.

Bernie gets to his feet, keeping the gun trained on Tom.

. . . There's one other thing I want. I wanna see Johnny Caspar cold and stiff. That's what you'll do for your friend Bernie.

He has opened the door to the flat.

. . . In the meantime I'll stay outta sight. But if Caspar ain't stiff in a couple of days—I start eating in restaurants.

The door shuts behind him.

Tom, heretofore very still, springs from the chair, goes to the bedroom, and grabs a gun.

He instinctively grabs his hat off the bedpost and, wearing only his boxer shorts, a sleeveless T-shirt, and the hat, he clambers out the open bedroom window.

FIRE ESCAPE

Tom trots down. His bare feet ring dully against the steel of the fire escape.

He reaches the bottom landing, swings over the railing, hangs by his hands for one brief moment, and then drops.

ALLEY

As Tom's bare feet hit the pavement. He straightens from his crouch and runs.

BACK DOOR

Over Tom's shoulder as he throws open his building's back door. The empty hall inside runs the length of the building to the front door, which is just closing.

We push Tom down the hall.

Before reaching the front door he falls violently forward.

His gun skates away across the floor.

He starts to roll over to look behind him and a crunching blow catches him on the chin, snapping his head the rest of the way around and sending him flat onto his back.

Bernie, who has emerged from under the staircase, towers over him.

BERNIE
You make me laugh, Tommy. You're gonna catch cold, then you're no good to me . . .

He is walking over to Tom's gun, which he picks up and unloads into his hand.

. . . What were you gonna do if you caught me? I'd just squirt a few and then you'd let me go again.

He tosses Tom the empty gun and walks out.

Tom, white-faced and shivering, pulls himself up to sit leaning against the wall.

A first-floor apartment door opens and elderly MRS. GRUBER *emerges, pulling a housecoat tight. She goggles at Tom.*

MRS. GRUBER

Why Mr. Reagan! What on earth . . .

Tom, in his underwear, tries on an idiotic smile.

TOM

They took everything.

LONG SHOT   THE HALL

Clucking sympathetically, the old woman leans down to help Tom up. As he drapes an arm over her stooped shoulders:

TOM

I fought like hell, but there were too many of 'em . . .

FADE OUT

CLOSE SHOT   PLAQUE

Set into an exterior wall, identifying the SHENANDOAH CLUB.

INT. LEO'S CLUB

Tom, in his overcoat and hat, is walking up to the bar.

TOM

'Lo, Tony. How's the club holding up?

Fat Tony looks sour.

TONY

We're managing to squeak by without you. Got Lazarre's money?

TOM

No.

TONY

Well, you're not supposed to be here since you turned rat.

TOM

Relax, Tony, Leo's not around is he?

TONY

Maybe Leo's not the only one doesn't care for you here.

Tom works to keep his smile.

TOM

. . . Fickle, huh, Tony? You could almost be a dame.

TONY

Pal, you read my mind, you speak my thoughts. Jesus, I hope you know what you're doing.

TOM

No more than usual. The last couple days, you booked any heavy bets on a long shot at Saturday's fights?

TONY

Why the hell should I tell you?

Tom shrugs.

TOM

The truth is, Tony, there's no reason on earth.

Staring at Tom, Tony blows air through his teeth. He sets up a drink for Tom.

TONY

. . . Saturday's fights. Yeah. Drop Johnson parked two yards on one yesterday. On Sailor Reese, an undercard bum.

Tom downs his drink in a gulp.

TOM
Drop Johnson? He play your book much?

TONY
You kidding? I didn't even know he could count.

From offscreen there is a loud CRASH and club patrons scream. Tom swivels to look as Tony looks off.

Oh, Jesus — you bring them with you?

Uniformed policemen are pouring into the club, wielding axes. They destroy everything in their path, sweeping elegantly dressed customers before them.

Tom wades into the sea of blue and nods at Delahanty, the policeman we know from the raid on Caspar's.

TOM
'Lo, Brian. Still fighting the good fight?

DELAHANTY
'Lo, Tom. Neither wind nor rain nor snow —

TOM
That's the mailmen. Is O'Doole here?

EXT. LEO'S CLUB

It is just cracking dawn.

O'Doole is leaning against a car, taking in the scene as he glumly chews a toothpick. The street is clogged with police vehicles.

Tom approaches.

TOM
'Lo, O'Doole. You don't look happy.

O'DOOLE
Look at this mess. Gutting the golden calf again.

He shakes his head.

. . . I don't know whether to laugh or cry.

244

TOM

Yeah, it's awful confusing. You know a yegg named Drop Johnson?

O'DOOLE

We've spanked him a couple times.

TOM

Where does he flop?

O'DOOLE

The Terminal Hotel on Bay Street, whenever he's broke – which is one hundred percent of always. Jesus . . .

He reacts to gunfire from the second story of the club.

. . . Don't nobody ask me, since I'm only the chief around here, but I'll tell you my opinion: Caspar's just as crazy as Leo. And an eye-tie into the bargain.

As he heads off:

TOM

What's the matter, O'Doole, doesn't anything ever suit you?

PULLING TOM

He walks along a nearby street; we can faintly hear the sirens and police activity back at the club.

A black touring car is tooling up alongside him. Tic-Tac leans out the driver's window. He has welts around his mouth; he has been roughed up.

TIC-TAC

Hop in, Tom, we been lookin' for you.

Briskly walking:

TOM

I'm busy.

TIC-TAC

Hop in anyway, as in you ain't got no choice.

TOM

You can't hijack me, Tic-Tac, we're on the same side now—or didn't you get that far in school?

The car screeches over to put a wheel on the sidewalk and block Tom's way. The back door swings open and Frankie emerges to help Tom in. Like Tic-Tac, Frankie looks a little worked over.

Tom quickly sizes up the situation and decides to comply.

INT. CAR

As Tom sits into the back, next to Eddie Dane. Frankie slides in after him and the car starts moving.

DANE

How'd you get the fat lip?

TOM

Old war wound. Acts up around morons.

DANE

Very smart. What were you doing at the club? Talking things over with Leo?

TOM

Don't think so hard, Eddie, you might sprain something.

DANE

You're so goddamn smart. Except you ain't. I get you, smart guy, I know what you are. Straight as a corkscrew. Mr. Inside-Outsky. Like a goddamn bolshevik, picking up your orders from Yegg Central. You think you're so goddamn smart. You joined up with Caspar. You bumped Bernie Bernbaum. Down is up. Black is white. Well, I think you're half-smart. I think you were straight with your frail and queer with Johnny Caspar. And I think you'd sooner join the Ladies' League than gun a guy down.

His eyes narrow at Tom.

. . . Then I hear that these two geniuses never even saw this rub-out take place.

246

TIC-TAC
(*defensively*)

The boss just said have him do it, he didn't say nothing about —

DANE

Shut up. Or maybe you still got too many teeth.

Tic-Tac sulks. Eddie Dane turns and gazes out the window.

. . . Everyone's so goddamn smart. Well, we'll go to Miller's Crossing. And we'll see who's smart.

MILLER'S CROSSING

It is morning; the sun is now fully up. Eddie Dane and Tom walk side-by-side through the woods. Frankie and Tic-Tac walk several steps ahead of them, each off to one side, searching. Frankie is singing a Neapolitan song.

DANE

Y'understand if we don't find a stiff out here, we leave a fresh one.

Tom's shoulders are hunched and his hands are jammed into his overcoat pockets. He stares woodenly forward. The Dane laughs softly.

. . . Where're your friends when you need 'em, huh? Where's Leo now?

Tom tramps mechanically on. His eyes drift up.

HIS POV

Tracking. A canopy of leaves, sprinkled with sunlight.

We hear the unearthly groan of tree limbs.

TOM

He looks forward.

The Dane calls out:

247

DANE

Hey, Tic-Tac, ever notice how the snappy dialogue dries up once a guy starts soiling his union suit?

Tom tramps on.

HIS POV

The backs of Frankie and Tic-Tac as they walk on ahead. Frankie is still singing.

TOM

He looks stupidly at the Dane. He looks ahead.

He stops abruptly.

DANE

What.

Tom is still for a moment, then with jerky movements gets down on his knees, hugs a tree with one arm for support, and vomits.

The Dane watches him, then calls out to Frankie and Tic-Tac:

. . . Okay. There's nothing out here.

He grabs Tom's hat off his head and flings it away. He plants a foot against Tom's side and shoves him to the ground.

CLOSE ON TOM

As his face hits the ground.

The Dane's foot enters; he plants it on the side of Tom's neck to keep him pinned.

TOM'S POV

Skewed angle, from the ground.

Frankie is skipping back, singing.

DANE

Checking the open chamber of his gun. He snaps it shut.

As he levels the gun at Tom:

                              DANE
    Think about this, smart guy.

TOM

Closing his eyes.

From offscreen:

                         TIC-TAC
    Uh-oh, hankie time!

FRANKIE

He stops singing and turns to look.

TOM

The foot comes off his neck.

DANE

Looking toward Tic-Tac.

TIC-TAC

Taking a handkerchief out of his breast pocket and bringing it to his face as he looks at something on the ground in front of him.

DANE

He hauls Tom to his feet and pushes him toward Tic-Tac.

We track behind the two men as they approach Tic-Tac, and Frankie enters from the other side.

We cannot yet see what is on the ground in front of them.

Birds been at him.

Frankie is taking out a hankie as he draws near.

FRANKIE
Jesus Christ . . .

He looks up at Tom as Tom approaches.

Over Tom and the Dane's shoulders, stretching away from us, face-up, is a body. We cannot see much of its face; what we do see is pulp.

Tic-Tac is laughing incredulously.

TIC-TAC
I said put one in his brain, not in his stinking face!

EXTREME LONG SHOT

Four small men in overcoats and fedoras, looking down at the ground; they are dwarfed by the surrounding trees.

Very faintly we hear:

FRANKIE
I told you, Dane, we heard two shots . . .

QUICK FADE OUT

BUILDING FOYER

A beat-up panel in the entryway lists tenants' names and apartments opposite a row of buttons.

A hand coasts along the names and stops at JOHNSON, CLARENCE/4C, then moves away and presses two buzzers on the fifth floor.

After a beat, we hear the front door buzz open.

FOURTH-FLOOR HALLWAY

Tom walks up to 4C, unpocketing a gun. He gently tries the knob, which turns, and enters.

DROP'S APARTMENT

As Tom enters.

DROP JOHNSON *is sitting at a table in the living room, which also serves as kitchen and dining room. He is a large man with a thick neck, a low forehead, and vacant eyes.*

He is looking up at Tom, a spoonful of cereal frozen halfway to his mouth, a folded-back newspaper in his other hand, opened to the funnies.

> TOM
> 'Lo, Drop. How're the Katzenjammers?

> DROP
> *(uncomfortably)*
> 'Lo, Tom. What's the rumpus?

As he talks, Tom ambles around the apartment, bumping open doors, sticking his head in each room.

> TOM
> Had any visitors?

Drop's head swivels to follow Tom around the room; otherwise he does not move. He speaks cautiously:

> DROP
> No.

> TOM
> Not ever, Drop?

> DROP
> . . . Not lately.

> TOM
> Then you must be happy to see me.

251

Drop doesn't respond.

. . . So you didn't see Bernie Bernbaum, before he was shown across?

DROP

No.

TOM

. . . Seen him since?

Drop maintains a sullen silence.

Tom is picking up a hat from a clutter on top of a bureau.

. . . One last question, Drop. I hear you've got a lot of money on tomorrow's fight. Is that your bet, or did you place it for a friend?

DROP

No, uh . . . it's my bet. I just . . . I have a good feeling about that fight . . .

Tom's stroll through the apartment has brought him behind Drop's chair.

TOM

A good feeling, huh? When did the feeling return to your head?

Tom deposits the hat on Drop's head. Drop's eyes roll up to look at it, but otherwise he does not move.

The too-small hat sits ludicrously atop his head.

Tom heads for the door.

. . . You've outgrown that one. Must be all the thinking you've been doing . . .

He pauses with his hand on the knob.

. . . Tell Bernie something's come up. He has to get in touch. There'll be nothing stirring till I talk to him.

He slams the door.

EXT.   A CLUB – DAY

We are looking at a ground-floor window upon which is stenciled
SONS OF ERIN SOCIAL CLUB.

A topcoated man scurries into frame, knocks out a pane with the
grip of his gun, and tosses a small pipelike device inside. We pan
with him as he scurries across the street to reveal a line of cars,
police and civilian, parked along the far curb. No men are visible
except the scurrying man, who takes cover behind one of the cars.

SOCIAL CLUB

A beat. From inside we hear a pair of trotting footsteps –

BOOM! *The window blows out, spitting glass into the street, along*
with a large dark form.

THE STREET

Glass showers the pavement and a charred rag-doll of a body hits
hard, face down, and skids a couple feet. Smoke wisps from it.

THE CLUB

A lick of flame from the bomb is dying and heavy gray smoke is
billowing out.

THE STREET

Men cautiously rise from behind the cars – a lot of men. Some
wear police uniforms; some are civilians. All are armed.

THE CLUB

Billowing smoke.

THE STREET

The men watch and wait. A policeman calls through a bullhorn:

POLICEMAN
All right, anyone left in there come on out, grabbin' air.
You know the drill.

THE CLUB

After a beat, the front door swings open. A man emerges, one hand in the air, one holding a handkerchief over his mouth.

He walks into the middle of the street.

One of the civilians behind the cars fires.

The man takes the bullet in the chest and drops to the ground, where he twitches.

A ripple of laughter runs down the line of men. The man who fired, in the foreground, grins.

THE CLUB WINDOW

Pouring smoke.

With a RAT-A-TAT-TAT, muzzle flashes from inside illuminate the smoke.

THE STREET

Bullets chew up the cars and a few of the men; the others drop back down behind the cars and start returning fire.

THE WINDOW

It is a forbidding black hole in the exterior wall. A second tommy joins the first to pour lead into the street.

MAYOR'S OFFICE RECEPTION AREA

We are tracking in on a youngish SECRETARY.

Faintly, from a distance, we can still hear gunfire.

'Lo, Tom, where've you been hiding?

REVERSE

On Tom.

TOM

Hither and yon. The mayor in?

SECRETARY

With Mr. Caspar.

Tom heads for the door.

TOM

That's who I'm looking for. Scare me up some gargle, will
you?

SECRETARY

Surely. And I'll announce you.

As he opens the door:

TOM

Don't bother. I'm well-liked.

MAYOR'S OFFICE

*A grand, high-ceilinged place. Mayor Levander sits sputtering
behind his desk, his face turning purple. Caspar, sitting across
from him, is also turning purple. Sitting to one side are two
identical thirty-year-old men, apparently twins, mustachioed,
silent, mournful, their hands clasped over the hats in their laps,
wearing stiff new suits and old-fashioned collars.*

MAYOR

I can't do it, Johnny! I'll look ridiculous! Why, it simply
isn't done! *Assistants,* maybe—

CASPAR

For a mayor, you don't hear so hot! I said *head! Head* of
the assessor's office!

255

MAYOR

But there's two of 'em!

CASPAR

I can count! Co-heads!

MAYOR

Johnny, needless to say, this office will do anything in its power to assist you and your cousins. We did it for Leo, of course, on countless occasions—

CASPAR

Damn right—had every potato eater from County Cork on the public tit!

MAYOR

But there's a way we do things, hallowed by usage and consecrated by time! When we put people on the pad, when Leo was running things, we—

Caspar is furious:

CASPAR

Leo ain't running things! I ain't innarested in ancient history! I'm running things now!

MAYOR

Johnny, no one appreciates that more than I! I can give them jobs! I can give them *good* jobs! I can even give them jobs where they won't have to perform any work, where their lack of English will be no impediment! But I can't—

CASPAR

What is this, the high hat?!

The mayor mops his face with a handkerchief and looks beseechingly at Tom.

MAYOR

Tom, can you explain it to him? I can put them in public works, but I can't—

TOM

You can do whatever the hell Caspar tells you. I don't remember all this double-talk when Leo gave you an order.

256

The mayor is flabbergasted.

MAYOR

Tom! Jesus!

TOM

Stop whimpering and do as you're told.

CASPAR

You can start by gettin' outta here.

MAYOR

But Johnny, it's my office!

CASPAR

Get outta here! Take it on the heel and toe before I whack
you one!

*The mayor retreats and Caspar glares at the two men sitting to
the side.*

. . . You too, beat it!

The two men look at each other, then back at Caspar.

FIRST MAN

. . . Partiamo?

CASPAR

Yeah, go keep the mayor company. I'll take care of yas
later.

*The immigrants rise and leave the room. Caspar takes out a
handkerchief and wipes his brow.*

. . . Runnin' things. It ain't all gravy.

*The secretary enters with a tray holding a bottle of whiskey, a
soda siphon, and ice. She puts it on the mayor's desk and leaves.*

*We still hear faint gunfire and an occasional booming explosion
that rattles the office windows.*

TOM

What's the fireworks?

CASPAR

Knockin' over one of Leo's clubs. Sonofabitch just won't go belly-up . . . I'm sorry, kid. I heard about your little ride this morning.

Tom walks over to pour himself a drink.

TOM

Yeah, well, sorry don't fix things. We could just as easily've missed Bernie's corpse as stumbled over it, and I'd be dead now.

CASPAR

I know, I know. But it don't mean the Dane's up to anything. So, he heard some rumor Bernie ain't dead; those stories pop up, people seen Dillinger in eight states last week. So, he hears a story and he don't like you much anyway, so he decides to check it out—

TOM

Any stories about Bernie being alive, the Dane's made up himself.

CASPAR

Aw, you don't know that. It don't even make sense—why would he?

TOM

There could be a damn good reason, if you've got a fixed fight coming up. Do you?

Caspar squints at Tom.

CASPAR

. . . Maybe. Okay, yeah, sure. Tomorrow night, the fix is in. What of it?

TOM

The Dane knows about it?

CASPAR

Yeah . . .

He gazes off.

. . . Okay, I get it.

TOM

If Eddie Dane's been selling you out on these fights, and means to again, he'll have to be able to point the finger at someone else—

CASPAR
(*uncomfortably*)

Yeah, yeah, I get it.

TOM

—but with Bernie dead there ain't a hell of a lot of people he can point to.

CASPAR

Yeah. The Dane sells me out. Makes pretend Bernie's still doin' it. At's real pretty. Bernie leaked the fix, and you take the fall for supposedly not killing him . . .

He leans back in the mayor's chair and gazes off, sucking his lips in and out as he thinks. Finally:

. . . But I dunno, why would Eddie cross me like that?— Money, okay, everybody likes money. But somehow it don't seem like him. And I know the Dane.

TOM

Nobody knows anybody. Not that well.

Caspar shakes his head.

CASPAR

Money don't mean that much to him.

Tom shrugs.

TOM

Then it's not just money he's after. He's got a wart on his fanny.

CASPAR

. . . Huh?

TOM

A wart. On his fanny. Giving him the fidgets. Maybe he's sick of sitting on the couch and maybe behind your desk don't look like a bad place to move to.

259

Caspar studies Tom.

CASPAR

. . . Kid, you got a lip on ya.

He looks off again.

. . . I don't generally care for it. But you're honest, and that's something we can't get enough of in this business. I'll admit, since last we jawed, my stomach's been seizin' up on me. The Dane saying we should double-cross you; you double-cross once, where's it all end? An innaresting ethical question.

He sighs.

. . . I'll find the Dane, talk to him, straighten it out—

Tom laughs bitterly.

TOM

Sure, talk to him. Have a chat. Ask him whether he's selling you out. Don't take care of him before he makes his next move, just sit back and let him make it. You're swimmin' in it.

Caspar's eyes flash. Tom adjusts his tone:

. . . Johnny, my chin's hanging out right alongside yours.

Caspar goes slack.

CASPAR

. . . Yeah.

TOM

I'd worry a lot less if I thought you were worrying enough.

Caspar, miserable, rubs his face. From the distant street we hear another booming explosion.

CASPAR

. . . But I am, kid . . . Christ . . . running things . . .

TOM'S APARTMENT – DUSK

The phone is ringing at the cut.

We are looking at the window sill upon which the phone sits, with an empty chair facing. Footsteps approach and Tom sits into frame and picks up the phone.

TOM

Yeah?

VOICE

I got your message.

TOM

'Lo, Bernie, I had a dream about you the other day.

We hear Bernie laugh.

BERNIE

. . . Yeah? A nightmare?

TOM

On the contrary; very sweet. I dreamt you were lying out at Miller's Crossing with your face blown off.

More laughter.

BERNIE

. . . You get a kick out of that?

TOM

I was in stitches. It's Mink, isn't it?

BERNIE

I came back and he wasn't happy to see me. Can you beat that, Tom?

TOM

Some friend.

BERNIE

Yeah. And you know what a nervous boy he was. I figured, hell, *you're* a friend. Maybe you could use some insurance.

TOM

That's you to the gills, Bernie: thoughtful. Did Mink have
a twenty-two?

BERNIE

He'd already ditched it. Why?

A moment's hesitation:

TOM

. . . After Rug?

BERNIE

Yeah . . . How did you know?

Down to business:

TOM

Doesn't matter. Listen, Bernie, I've been thinking about
our little deal and I've decided you can stick it in your ear.

BERNIE

. . . Huh?

TOM

I figure you don't have anything on me that I don't have
on you, so I'm calling your bluff.

BERNIE

Wait a minute —

TOM

Shut up and let me talk. I'm pulling out of here,
tomorrow morning. The only thing for you to decide is
whether or not I leave behind a message for Caspar that
you're still around. If you want me to keep my mouth
shut, it'll cost you some dough.

BERNIE

You can't —

TOM

I figure a thousand bucks is reasonable. So I want two
thousand.

> BERNIE

In a pig's eye—

> TOM

I'm going out for a while; I'll be back here at four this morning. Bring me the money. If you're not at my place, four o'clock, with the dough, Caspar'll be looking for you tomorrow.

He hangs up on Bernie's sputtering.

TOM'S HALLWAY

We are close on Tom as, in overcoat and hat, he emerges from his apartment and looks down at the keys in his hand.

WHAP—a fist swings into frame to connect with Tom's cheek. He falls back.

Three topcoated men loom over him.

> FIRST MAN

Got any money?

Tom massages his face.

> TOM

No.

The first man nods to the other two.

> FIRST MAN

Okay.

The two men pick Tom off the floor and start to work him over. He doesn't resist.

The first man watches dispassionately.

. . . Third race tonight. By the finish, Tailor Maid had a view of the field.

He lights himself a cigarette.

. . . You oughta lay off the ponies, Tom.

The two men work in silence for a while. Tom too is silent.

263

Finally:
> . . . Okay.

The two men release Tom and back away, breathing heavily. Tom slides down the wall to the floor.
> . . . Lazarre said he's sorry about this. It's just getting out of hand.

Tom speaks thickly, his head propped against the baseboard:

TOM
> . . . Yeah.

FIRST MAN
> He likes you, Tom. He said we didn't have to break anything.

TOM
> Yeah. Tell him no hard feelings.

FIRST MAN
> Christ, Tom, he knows that.

With a jerk of the head the first man signals the other two and the trio turns to leave.
> . . . Take care now.

CASPAR'S DOORWAY – NIGHT

We are looking over Tom's shoulder as he waits in the rain in front of a large oak doorway with wrought-iron fretwork. At the cut we hear chimes dying, and the door swings open.

There is a grand foyer with a parquet floor, unsittable furniture, and a large chandelier. A liveried BUTLER *looks inquiringly out.*

TOM
> Tom Reagan.

BUTLER
> Yes, sir . . .

He steps back.
> . . . Mr. Caspar is in the great room.

Tom hands the butler his hat.

TOM

Swell. Can you hold this?

As Tom starts to shrug out of his coat, Caspar is entering the foyer. His greeting is listless:

CASPAR

Kid, what's the rumpus.

TOM

I got news.

CASPAR

Yeah, news at this end too. My stomach's been seizin' up on me.

TOM

Mink just told me that he –

This wakes Caspar up:

CASPAR

You talked to Mink?!

TOM

Yeah, on the phone. The Dane wants you to think he's disappeared so you can't talk to him, but he's been right here in town.

CASPAR

You're sure it was Mink?

Tom shrugs.

TOM

See for yourself; he's coming to my place, four o'clock this morning . . .

Having handed the butler his hat and coat, Tom lets Caspar lead him toward a pair of double doors.

. . . He's afraid of a cross from the Dane. He told me about the fix. Says he'll sing for a couple grand skip money, tell us everyone involved . . .

Caspar opens one of the double doors and we continue tracking behind the two men as they enter a trophy room.

The room has the low warm light of a men's club. Outside its dark windows, rain sheets down.

Caspar sits in behind his desk and swivels away to poke morosely with a shovel at the blaze in the fireplace. In the foreground, back to us, Tom rests his knuckles on the desk to lean in toward Caspar.

. . . But you better take care of the Dane right away. Mink says he's coming after us tonight.

As he looks glumly into the fire:

CASPAR
Leo's holed up at Whiskey Nick Paraskevetes' dump.

Tom is momentarily taken aback.

TOM
. . . How d'you know?

From behind him, a chuckle.

REVERSE

On Tom. Behind him, Eddie Dane is walking over to close the door.

DANE
That ain't all we know, smart guy.

He points with a nod to the couch.

. . . Recognize your playmate?

On the couch sits Drop Johnson. Drop's face looks worked on, and is beaded over with sweat.

Having shut the door, the Dane is sauntering over to Tom.

. . . Yeah. You thought I'd quit.

He shakes his head.

Huh-uh. I followed you this afternoon. And I wondered why Einstein would want to talk to a gorilla . . .

266

He is nose to nose with Tom, smiling at him.

. . . So I grabbed the gorilla. And I beat it out of him.

He shrugs.

. . . Give me a big guy, every time. They crack easy. Not like you.

Tom holds Eddie Dane's look.

TOM
Is there a point? Or are you just brushing up on your small talk?

DANE
I like that. Cool under fire. I'm impressed.

Quickly he delivers two slaps—forehand and backhand. Tom's head rocks, but he recovers to stare back at the Dane.

. . . The gorilla didn't know whose stiff we found, but I can fill that in. You killed Mink, you sonofabitch.

He grabs Tom by the lapels, swings him away from the desk, and lands a punch on his chin. Tom stumbles back.

Caspar has turned from the fireplace to watch.

Eddie Dane moves toward Tom, breathing hard with anticipated pleasure.

. . . Come here, bum. I'm gonna send you to a deep dark place. And I'm gonna have fun doing it.

The Dane grabs Tom by the front of the coat and hauls him close. He slaps him savagely.

It was Mink, and by God I'll hear you say it!

TOM
Is this how you taught Drop his story?

The Dane's hands wrap around Tom's throat, choking him off. As the pressure increases, Tom, purpling, sinks to his knees.

DANE
I like the way you think. Maybe when you're dead I'll cut your head off, put it on my mantelpiece—

WHANG—*a shovel blade swings into frame to smash the Dane's face.*

He drops.

From somewhere in the room, a scream.

Eddie Dane is on his hands and knees, one hand pressed over his ruined face, blood pouring between the fingers.

CASPAR

Sonofabitch . . .

He stands over Eddie Dane with the fireplace shovel.

. . . If there's one thing I can't stand, it's a double-cross artist! I had a feeling 'bout this sonofabitch—

He swings the shovel back and delivers an overhand blow to the top of the Dane's head.

The Dane drops to the floor, instantly motionless.

The scream, however, continues.

Drop Johnson, on the couch, eyes wide, hands spastically squeezing his knees, is looking down at the Dane. Drop's mouth is stretched wide. He is screaming.

Tom gets slowly to his feet.

Caspar looks at Drop.

. . . Shut it, you sonofabitch!

He is striding over with the shovel.

. . . I'll give you something to holler about!

Tom intercepts him.

> TOM
>
> Johnny. It's okay. The Dane made him. It's okay. It's not important.

Caspar is panting.

> CASPAR
>
> Then have him shut it!

Drop does.

There is a beat.

Incongruously, Caspar's bellow breaks the silence:

. . . And we do the same to Mink! This very same night!

Another silence. The rain. The crackle of the fire.

Tom's tone is soothing:

> TOM
>
> Johnny. We can't double-cross Mink. He wants to spill the whole set-up –

Caspar stares at him through glazed eyes.

> CASPAR
>
> I've never let a sonofabitch walk!

> TOM
>
> You've never crossed anyone . . .

Caspar is staring at him. His eyes begin to focus.

. . . Four o'clock, my place. Mink's coming in on his own hook, so I promised him the money. Don't make me out a liar—

Suddenly Drop is screaming again.

Caspar looks where Drop is looking:

Eddie Dane is lifting his head, moaning. His face is a mask of blood. One hand gropes in his overcoat pocket for his gun.

Caspar shouts over Drop's howl as he pulls something from his desk drawer:

CASPAR

Lookit this, kid . . .

He strides over to the Dane.

. . . Something I try and teach all my boys . . .

With the gun point blank against the back of the Dane's head, he fires.

Tom recoils.

. . . Always put one inna brain!

A WALL CLOCK

Cut in to quiet. It is 3:30.

We are pulling back and down to reveal that we are inside a diner; we are isolating on a section of counter upon which sit a half-empty cup of coffee and an ashtray half filled with butts. A hand puts some change on the counter and leaves frame.

EXT. DINER

As Tom exits. He tucks his overcoat collar up as he walks; it is still pouring rain.

Tom turns at the sound of approaching heels and, with surprise, recognizes Verna. She doesn't seem to much notice the rain.

TOM

'Lo, Verna. What's the rumpus.

Coldly, as they walk on together:

> VERNA
>
> I was just in the neighborhood, feeling a little daffy. What're you doing?

> TOM
>
> . . . Walking.

> VERNA
>
> Don't let on more than you have to.

> TOM
>
> In the rain.

Tom glances at her.

> . . . What're you doing out?

> VERNA
>
> Bernie's dead, isn't he?

They walk on for a beat, Tom looking down at the sidewalk. Finally:

> TOM
>
> . . . What makes you think that?

> VERNA
>
> That's no answer.

Tom glances around and pulls Verna into a dark alcove. It is small; they have to crowd into each other to stay out of the rain. Water drips from the brim of Tom's fedora. He studies Verna for a beat.

> TOM
>
> I can't tell you anything yet.

> VERNA
>
> Nobody cares, do they? His friends didn't really like him.

Tom shrugs.

> TOM
>
> He didn't like his friends.

VERNA

You're a sonofabitch, Tom. You're someone to talk. You got me to tell you where he was and then you killed him.

She raises a gun into frame and presses it into his stomach.

Tom stiffens but continues to look at her calmly.

. . . Tell me why. What was in it for you?

TOM

Nothing for me.

VERNA

Then why?

TOM

Giving up Bernie was the only way I could see to straighten things out for Leo.

VERNA

You said you didn't care about Leo.

TOM

I said we were through. It's not the same thing.

Verna looks at him.

VERNA

. . . I don't understand. I don't care. I don't care what reasons you had or thought you had.

She raises the gun and presses its barrel into the underside of Tom's chin.

TOM

. . . He's still alive.

Verna stares at him.

VERNA

You expect me to believe you?

TOM

. . . No.

VERNA

That's you all over, Tom. A lie and no heart.

Verna pulls back the hammer. There is a long beat.

Verna's eyes widen, locked on Tom's.

Tom returns her look; his is sympathetic.

Verna starts trembling.

Tom's tone is soft:

TOM

   . . . It isn't easy, is it, Verna?

She abruptly lurches away and staggers a couple of paces out into the rain. She hugs a lamp post for support. She is staring down at the street, trembling.

Tom walks up behind her and rests a hand on her shoulder.

   . . . Are you all right?

She doesn't look around.

VERNA

   . . . I don't know how you did it.

She shrugs off his hand and stumbles off down the street.

Tom watches her go.

TREE LIMBS

Night, but some time later—it has stopped raining. The branches groan in the wind. Street light glitters off the leaves, still wet with rain.

We are booming down to reveal that we are in front of Tom's building, its windows dark. Throughout the boom down we hear the rumble of an approaching car and the hiss of its tires on wet asphalt.

The car pulls into frame to stop at the curb as the boom down ends, framed up on the driver's window. The DRIVER *has a small bandage on his left cheek. We hear Caspar's voice as he climbs out the back:*

CASPAR

Ya put the razor in cold water, not hot — 'cause metal does what in cold?

DRIVER

I dunno, Johnny.

We hear the back door slam and Caspar appears in the front passenger window.

CASPAR

. . . At's what I'm tellin' ya. It contracts. At way you get a first-class shave.

DRIVER

Okay, Johnny.

As Caspar walks off the driver slouches back, pulls his fedora over his eyes, and folds his arms across his chest.

. . . Ain't it the life, though.

A back enters frame in the foreground.

TOM'S VOICE

'Lo, Sal. You can dangle.

The driver looks up, startled.

DRIVER

'Lo, Tom. You sure? You don't look so hot.

TOM

I'm okay. Go ahead, I'll drive him home.

The driver shrugs.

REVERSE

Wider, from the other side of the car as it pulls away.

Tom walks into the foreground, toward his house; we tilt up to hold him.

The low angle shows us the tree behind Tom, its branches still creaking in the wind.

CRACK, CRACK — *we hear two gunshots from inside the house. Tom stops momentarily in close shot, looking up, and then continues on out of frame.*

OVER TOM'S SHOULDER

We follow him as he walks into the building and down the first-floor hall.

The hallway is quiet except for a light moaning wind.

Beyond Tom we see the door to the first-floor apartment crack open.

HISSING VOICE
Mr. Reagan . . .

The door opens wider. Mrs. Gruber, wearing a housecoat, her gray hair down in braids, sticks her head out.

. . . There were shots.

Tom looks up toward the staircase.

TOM
Go down to the drugstore. Call the police.

She stares at him, nods, and drapes on a raincoat.

MRS. GRUBER
Yes, Mr. Reagan.

TOM
You better stay there till the officers arrive.

MRS. GRUBER
Yes . . .

She pauses.

. . . Will my cats be all right?

Tom stares at her.

Finally, he nods.

TOM
. . . They'll be fine.

Mrs. Gruber returns his dazed nod and shuffles away.

So far, upstairs, all is quiet.

PULLING TOM

As he starts slowly toward the staircase.

HIS POV   TRACKING FORWARD

A small black object rests on the staircase — an upside-down fedora.

Blood drips with a hollow rattle down onto a stair tread, a couple steps above the hat.

PULLING TOM

He looks up.

HIS POV

A head sticks through the balusters of the second-story landing return. The body is on its back; the head lolls back, over the lip of the landing, down toward the stairs.

Our climbing low angle shows us mostly the back of the head. The body's far shoulder has knocked out a baluster whose splintered bottom juts out at a jagged angle.

PULLING TOM

Climbing, looking at the body.

HIS POV

Climbing and panning as we draw even with the head.

It is Caspar. Blood has been expelled through his nostrils over his mouth and chin. His face is deep red. His eyes stare glassily at Tom.

PULLING TOM

As he reaches the top of the stairs and swings around to face along the landing. We hear a chuckle, close by. Wind groans through the hallway.

TOM'S POV

In the middle foreground Caspar lies on the floor; beyond him, Bernie leans against the frame of Tom's open doorway, smiling, his arms folded over his chest.

The balusters stretch away in a regular line, throwing vertical shadows up against the opposite wall.

BERNIE

I get it. You set me up. Anything to avoid a little dirty work yourself, huh?

Tom doesn't answer. He leans against the wall and looks morosely down at Caspar

. . . How'd you know he'd get it and not me? Or didn't you care?

Tom shrugs, still staring down at the body.

TOM

I figured you'd come early, and be looking for blood. He wouldn't, so you'd likely have the drop on him.

BERNIE

You're a sonofabitch, Tom. I like the way you think. You're right, the chump never knew what hit him.

He looks down at Caspar, unable to suppress a smile.

. . . But if you knew I'd come looking to kill you, how do you know I won't still?

Tom shrugs again.

TOM

Nothing in it for you, now. With him dead we got nothing on each other. Let me have the gun.

277

BERNIE
Why?

Tom jerks his head toward Caspar.

TOM
Pin this on the Dane. Neither of us want him walking
around after this.

BERNIE
The cops'll be Leo's now. They won't care what they hang
the Dane for.

Tom shrugs again.

TOM
I guess that's so. If you don't mind keeping the gun that
killed Caspar. And Mink.

*He stoops down over Caspar's body and starts feeling through
Caspar's pockets, looking for something.*

. . . Why did Mink shoot Rug, anyway?

BERNIE
I dunno, it was just a mix-up. Here.

*Tom looks back over his shoulder. Bernie hands him his gun,
which Tom slips into his overcoat pocket.*

. . . So you're gonna say the Dane did this?

As he goes back to the body:

TOM
Mink thought Rug was tailing him?

*He finds Caspar's gun and sets it on the floor, but continues his
search.*

BERNIE
Yeah, yeah, you know Mink. Hysterical. Skin full of hop,
head full of bogeymen. Comes home crying one day, said
he had to pop a guy, one of the Dane's spies.

TOM
Rug was following Verna, not Mink. Mink just happened
to be with her.

He has found a wallet and is thumbing through it.

BERNIE

Yeah. Funny, ain't it? But you know, Mink was terrified the Dane'd find out we were jungled up together.

Tom takes out the cash, riffles it, and replaces the wallet.

TOM

And I'll bet you'd kept him plenty worried about that, to keep him under your thumb.

BERNIE

Yeah, so what . . .

Bernie is peering over Tom's shoulder at the money.

. . . Scratch, huh? A little bonus?

Tom straightens up, Caspar's gun in hand.

TOM

Why did Mink take Rug's hair?

Bernie shrugs.

BERNIE

Beats me, the kid was dizzy. Fifty-fifty on the dough? Or maybe I should get a little more, since I did the deed . . .

Tom stuffs the money into his pocket.

. . . Okay, you keep it. I want you to have it.

TOM

Bernie . . .

He nods toward Caspar's body.

. . . we can't hang this on the Dane.

BERNIE

Huh? Why not?

TOM

The Dane's already dead, halfway 'cross town.

Bernie's smile fades.

279

BERNIE

What the hell are you talking about?

TOM

Eddie Dane is dead. It's gotta be you. I mean hell, it's your gun.

Alarm begins to rise:

BERNIE

What is this! What the hell are you talking about! . . .

He looks down at Caspar and then back at Tom.

. . . You *took* my gun! It's just your word against mine!

Tom pops the chamber of Caspar's gun, glances in, and snaps it shut.

TOM

Not necessarily.

Bernie's eyes widen.

BERNIE

Are you crazy? We're square! You said it yourself! We got nothing on each other!

TOM

Yup.

BERNIE

So what's in it for you?! There's no angle! You can't just shoot me, like that!

He sinks to his knees, his voice rising.

. . . Jesus Christ! It don't make sense! Tommy! Look in your heart!

TOM

What heart.

BANG—*Bernie splays backward from the knees, a bullet drilled neatly through his forehead.*

Tom drops the gun by Caspar's body.

He unpockets Bernie's gun, goes to Bernie's corpse, and drops it there.

We pan with Tom's legs to bring his doorway into view as he walks into his apartment, goes to the window chair in the background, and sits with his back to us.

The windows show daylight breaking. Far away a clock strikes the quarter hour.

Tom picks up the phone and dials. Waiting for an answer, he reaches over to turn off the feeble yellow lamp burning chairside.

As we fade out we hear:

TOM

. . . Tony? Tom. Tell Lazarre I've got his money . . . Yeah, all of it. And I want to place a bet on tonight's fight . . .

A BEAT OF BLACK

LEO'S HALLWAY

We are tracking over Tom's shoulder as he walks up the hall, led by Dead Terry.

TERRY

They set you up downstairs?

TOM

How's that?

TERRY

Hootch? Whatever?

Tom gestures with the drink he is carrying. Its ice cubes clink.

. . . Well thanks for coming, Tom. Leo's real anxious to see you.

TOM

I happened to be near.

We hear muffled bellowing from Leo's office, growing louder as we approach.

Terry seems embarrassed:

TERRY

Actually . . . this might not be the best time . . .

They have pulled up in front of the closed door to Leo's office.

Leo's bellowing, inside, abates for a moment. We hear another voice, muffled so that we don't hear the words but only their plaintive tone.

Leo's bellowing cuts it short.

TOM

. . . Who's he got in there?

TERRY

O'Doole and the mayor.

As he leaves frame:

TOM

I'll try again.

Terry calls after him:

TERRY

I'll tell him you stopped by.

DOWNSTAIRS

Pulling Tom as he walks across the gambling floor, drink still in hand. Behind him we can see workmen busily repairing the damage done to the club in the police raid.

Halfway across the floor Tom stiffens and slows, seeing something.

Verna is entering the club.

The two meet.

TOM

'Lo, Verna.

'Lo, Tom. See Leo?

They both lean against a countertop and look out at the floor.

TOM

He was busy.

VERNA

You should see him. He has something to tell you.

TOM

Maybe I'll run into him.

VERNA

Bernie's funeral is tomorrow. You could stop by.

TOM

Maybe.

VERNA

. . . Leo has something to tell you.

TOM

So you said.

There is a silent beat. Verna scowls.

VERNA

. . . Tell me something, Tom. Why didn't you tell me
what was going on? I thought he was dead, and you
never—

TOM

There was no point in telling you. It could only have
queered things if it had gotten out—

VERNA

Jesus, Tom! You don't just talk to people for the play it
gives you or doesn't give you! I suffered, you no-heart son
of a bitch!

Tom lets this drift.

Verna tries to compose herself.

. . . I'm sorry. It's just that things might've been different. With us. If I'd known that you hadn't . . . done anything to him . . .

TOM

You know now.

Verna looks at him.

VERNA

What happened that night?

Tom looks at her evenly.

TOM

I went to a bar. Passed out. When I got back to my place they were both dead.

Verna studies him.

VERNA

. . . Passed out, huh?

TOM

Yeah.

She looks at him a beat longer, then out at the floor.

VERNA

It's funny, I've never even seen you sleep – though you told me once about a dream you had.

TOM

Maybe I lied.

WHAP! Verna slaps him hard. His head rocks under the blow.

VERNA

You've never been straight with me about anything! You *are* a sonofabitch!

Tom watches her go.

He raises the drink and rolls it across his slapped cheek.

The ice cubes clink.

284

CEMETERY

A small old marble orchard on a hilltop cleared against the woods. Stars of David adorn the headstones; in the foreground Bernie's funeral is ending. Present is a rabbi, just finishing the chanting of the liturgy, Verna, and Leo.

In the background, on the road at the foot of the hill, Tom emerges from a taxi. It rolls away as he starts up the hill. Just as he arrives, Leo and Verna turn to leave.

Tom takes in the scene.

                    TOM
   Big turnout.

                    VERNA
   Drop dead.

She stalks off, leaving Leo and Tom alone. Leo takes off his yarmulke and fiddles with it uncomfortably. The two men start walking.

                    LEO
   . . . She's under a lot of strain.

                    TOM
   Well, at least she didn't hit me.

Leo chuckles.

They walk on.

                    LEO
   Tommy, I'm glad you came—

                    TOM
   She's taking the car.

                    LEO
   —Huh?

Leo looks up.

Verna is getting into the elegant black touring car that waits at the bottom of the hill. It pulls away.

Leo looks at Tom.

. . . I guess we're walking.

TOM

I guess we are.

They walk in silence for a beat.

LEO

. . . We're getting married.

Tom stiffens. He brings out:

TOM

. . . Congratulations.

Leo too is uncomfortable.

LEO

The funny thing is . . . *she* asked *me*. To tie the knot. I guess you're not supposed to say that.

TOM

It doesn't matter. Congratulations.

LEO

Thanks . . . Hell, Tom! Why didn't you tell me what you were up to?! I thought you'd really gone over – not that I didn't deserve it. But you could have told me!

TOM

Telling you could only've queered things if it had . . .

Tom cuts himself off and walks in silence for a beat.

. . . There just wasn't any point.

Leo wants to be encouraging. He nods.

LEO

I can see that. Well. It was a smart play, all around. I guess you know I'm grateful.

TOM

No need.

Leo is grinning again.

286

LEO

I guess you picked that fight with me just to tuck yourself in with Caspar.

TOM

I dunno. Do you always know why you do things, Leo?

Leo greets this with a puzzled smile.

LEO

Course I do.

He nods to himself.

. . . It was a smart play.

They walk on.

Leo stops, grabs Tom's arm, and the words come out in a rush:

. . . Jesus, Tom! I'd give anything if you'd work for me again. I know I've made some bonehead plays! I know I can be pig-headed but, damnit, so can you! I need your help, and things can be like they were, I know it! I just know it! As for you and Verna—well, I understand, you're both young, and—well, damnit, Tom, I forgive you!

Tom bristles. For the first time his tone is sharp:

TOM
I didn't ask for that and I don't want it.

The two men stare at each other—Tom's look angry; Leo's, distraught.

Tom's look softens.

. . . Goodbye, Leo.

Leo stares at him, waiting for something else. When nothing comes, he turns, and walks away.

Tom watches him go. He takes out a flask, pops its cap, drinks. He recaps it and pockets it, his eyes on the road.

Behind him a tree soughs in the wind.